SOCIAL IDEALS IN GERMAN LITERATURE

1770-1830

SOCIAL IDEALS IN GERMAN LITERATURE

1770-1830

BY

LUDWIG W. KAHN

AMS PRESS
NEW YORK

Reprinted with the permission of
Columbia University Press
From the edition of 1938, New York
First AMS EDITION published 1969
Manufactured in the United States of America

Library of Congress Catalogue Card Number: 75-84876

AMS PRESS, INC.
New York, N.Y. 10003

CONTENTS

SOCIAL IDEALS IN GERMAN LITERATURE
1770-1830

I

INTRODUCTION

"SOCIAL IDEALS," as the term is used in the present study, refers to the poet's conception of the way in which men should live together and what their mutual relations should be. Comparatively little attention is devoted to theoretical statements on the subject, the chief emphasis being placed on the ideals implicit in the poetry, fiction, and drama of writers who may not, indeed, have been consciously aware of them.

Thus, the revolt against conventions and traditions may be regarded as a social ideal. But very often such revolt will find expression not only in the actual and empirical sphere of society but also in religion; indeed, this revolt can be so much a part of the character and ethics of an individual that it reflects his relationship not to his fellowmen but primarily to himself and to God. Similarly, such conceptions as "freedom," "duty," "law," can refer to ultimate decisions which the individual must reach by himself with no reference to other persons. Some readers may object, therefore, that the term "social ideals" is given too broad an interpretation, embracing as it does here not only political, economic, or social ideals in the narrowest sense but also the religious, ethical and pedagogical elements which are often inherent and sometimes predominant in such ideals. But the very fact that the social ideals of most of the poets treated in the pages of this book cannot and must not be separated from the profound metaphysical problems in which they were absorbed would appear to justify an investigation of this complex question.

The following chapters are an attempt to trace the principal development in these ideals and thus to contribute in some measure to the history of ideas. But at the same time, by relating the ideals to such movements as "classicism" and "romanticism," terms which of late have been used to denote stylistic and formalistic tendencies, the author wishes to point out the interdependence of form and content, of a history of ideas and a history of style.

The method used in this book of comparing and contrasting one poem with another (or what in principle is the same— of comparing a poem with a type, even a bogus type), may easily lead to abstractions and hairsplitting. At the same time, however, such types serve to clarify points in question and to facilitate literary analysis. For it is only after a fundamental direction has been determined that it is possible to follow sidetracks, twisted and tangled byways, without being hopelessly lost in a labyrinth. But it is well to remember, too, that in the history of ideas there are no watertight compartments, no clear-cut demarcations, and that, having established certain directions, we must allow for certain deviations and exceptions. The author trusts that he has not forced his thesis unduly, for he is aware that in each period many a quotation could be found to invalidate his simple array of types. Any general classification must necessarily be somewhat unjust to the individual case.

Generally speaking, the history of ideas is a continuous process, and the change from one idea to another is merely a gradual one. Inevitably there must be borderline cases and overlappings. And there are, of course, as in every age, scores of poems which express no social ideal at all. The present study of important tendencies, written as it is from a special point of view, is intended in no way as an exhaustive analysis of the works discussed in the following chapters.

STURM-UND-DRANG: INDIVIDUALISM

THE ETERNAL CONFLICT BETWEEN THE INDIVIDUAL AND SOCIETY

ACCORDING to the conception of tragedy which gained wide acceptance during the classical period of German literature, a tragic occurrence must be of exemplary and general concern. A merely incidental disaster, therefore, is not a tragedy. Lessing's *Emilia Galotti,* when viewed from this approach, appears to recount a series of unfortunate coincidences which eventuate in disaster but which lack absolute necessity. For if the prince had had a higher sense of duty, or if he had been a constitutional monarch, or if there had been a democratic instead of an autocratic government, the conflict would probably not have arisen at all. In fact, the conflict has its origin in a defect of society which Lessing seeks to bring to light and ultimately to remedy. He is motivated by reformist tendencies, and his play reflects a new sense of social responsibility in that it is an indictment of the tyranny of princes and a passionate plea for the Rights of Man. Lessing sets out, in fact, to prove that the misfortunes he depicts are avoidable and must be avoided, and it is for this reason that he fails to impart the conviction of compelling and immutable necessity characteristic of classical tragedy.[1]

Many of the plays of the Sturm-und-Drang are still inspired by this passion for social reform, but in some the conflict between the individual and society becomes inevitable, irreconcilable, and fatal. For, unlike Lessing and the rationalists, the Stürmer-und-Dränger fought not for the abolition of specific abuses or for a just social order, but for the complete emancipation of the individual—an aim which comes into conflict with society not only here and now, but always and everywhere. Individualism becomes so extreme and radical that its antipathy to society is absolute and eternal.

This explains perhaps the rather puzzling denouement of Schiller's *Räuber*. Schiller cannot have intended that Karl Moor should admit himself in the wrong and make amends for his action, for such an attitude would have detracted from the pathos of the play. Instead Karl recognizes the eternal incompatibility of his demand for entirely free action and self-fulfillment with the claims of society. The reader is left with the feeling that the utterly destructive conflict between society and the individual is tragic because it is unavoidable. Karl Moor is not the victim of his villainous brother, or of social injustice, as Emilia Galotti is the victim of the prince. The wrongs Karl suffers are only the forces which cause him to put individualism into practice; and he perishes because individualism and society are forever antagonistic. Karl not only fails to find the greatness and freedom of which he had dreamed, but he is awakened to the knowledge that greatness cannot and never will be accorded to him or to anyone else.

The theme of "Bruderkampf" permeates Klinger's *Die Zwillinge* as it does Schiller's *Räuber*. Guelfo finds himself hampered in the expression of his individuality; he feels that his energy is paralyzed, his ambition thwarted, his strong nature deprived of its due scope, while his merits are unrecognized, and the rights to which he lays claims denied him. And he believes specifically that his brother stands in his way:

Ich bin nur Guelfo—ein Mensch, der wegen seiner Taten schrecklich unter Freunden und Feinden ist. Da ist Ferdinando, ein eitles, schwaches, elendes, püppisches Männchen, der von Empfindsamkeit viel schwätzt, nichts als ein bisschen Mädchenseele hat.

He derives support for his attitude from the even gloomier Grimaldi:

Noch einmal, was mich ärgert, ist, dass du zur Eiche aufgewachsen warst, nun dastehst, ein kleines dürres Bäumchen am Wege, für das der Bettler ebenso wenig Ehrfurcht hat als der Grosse, und jeder dich anstösst, sich ein Sprösschen abbricht, dass du kahl dastehest.

Guelfo considers himself an exceptional man and demands exceptional rights. Finally he kills his brother; like Karl Moor he refuses to repent his action and to establish by his death the superiority of the law, as a hero of Schiller's classical plays would have done. Klinger's *Zwillinge* is another illustration of the incompatibility of individual and society.

How well Klinger succeeded in expressing this conviction of frustration, of being slighted by life and thwarted in the struggle for self-fulfillment, may be seen from the impression his play made on the hero of K. P. Moritz's *Anton Reiser:*[2]

Guelfo glaubte sich von der Wiege an unterdrückt—das glaubte er (Reiser) von sich auch—ihm fielen dabei alle die Demütigungen und Kränkungen ein, denen er von seiner frühsten Kindheit an, fast so lange er denken konnte, beständig ausgesetzt worden war.

The more intense the individualism, the more inevitable becomes its conflict with society, or indeed with any limitation from without. Thus, a certain strain of "Weltschmerz," of pessimism and weariness, is implicit in Sturm-und-Drang. The world is regarded as a prison in which the individual is confined, and only death can solve the conflict between the individual and the world. This attitude is particularly striking in Goethe's *Goetz.*

THE RIGHTS OF THE INDIVIDUAL

The individual who, despite a heroic struggle, is eventually crushed by society is the favorite subject of Sturm-und-Drang. And there is no doubt that to the poets of this movement society is wrong and the individual is right. Society cripples the individual and interferes with his happiness.

The poet aligns himself with the individual, looking toward the ideal state in which the individual is absolutely free, a law unto himself.

When Julius von Tarent, in Leisewitz's play, sets out to live his own life, his friend and confidant Aspermonte reminds him of his obligations as a prince toward the state and society. Julius replies: "(Die Gesellschaft setzt) Fürsten und Nonnen und zwischen beiden eine Kluft . . . Der Staat tötet die Freiheit." Just as Julius declares himself free of all demands which society may make upon him, Brother Martin (in *Goetz*) protests against the monastic vows which clash with the natural instincts and impulses of the individual. Lenz, too, in *Die Soldaten*, pens a diatribe against the unnatural celibacy imposed upon soldiers.

The famous slogan "Back to Nature," as understood by this generation, meant primarily opposition to every convention of society, from fashion in clothing to principles of morality. Everything dictated from without—style, pattern, or precedent—was an infringement of the individual's liberty. "To follow one's nature" or "to live a natural life" was equivalent to gratifying one's impulses. The admiration for the "savage" reflected what amounted to envy of a man unspoiled by society, free to follow his inclinations, whose individuality remained unfettered by external restrictions. The Sturm-und-Drang glorifies "den ganzen Kerl," the vigorous man who eschews delicate language and in every way performs all kinds of marvels of strength. The subjects of Klinger's play, *Sturm-und-Drang*, show by their very names ("Wild," "Le Feu") that they really *are* "characters." It is the right and duty of the superman to express his individuality. The extraordinary man has extraordinary rights. Fiesco, for example, claims markedly exceptional prerogatives: when he recounts to his fellow-citizens the parable of the animal king, he not only suggests to them that the role of

the lion properly belongs to him, but he seeks also to convince
himself of his title to the throne. Fiesco, too, is aware of the
eternal incompatibility between the claims of the individual
and the resistance presented by the world. On the other hand,
it is noteworthy that Schiller does not side unequivocally
with Fiesco.

SELF-ASSERTION IN LOVE

The individual must be true to his own self; he must allow
no consideration for others, not even love, to confine him to
a position in which his nature will not be permitted widest
scope. Klinger's *Simsone Grisaldo* presents a hero who is a
brave, magnanimous, yet simple general, a repository of the
massed strength of his people. It is his natural bent to be a
soldier and to advance steadily from victory to victory, and
he must take pains not to be diverted from a way of life
which thus expresses his individuality. Grisaldo considers it
his right to take any girl who catches his fancy and then to
pass on to other conquests; he must fulfill his desires, and
the women who love him and are abandoned by him accept
his inconstancy and love him in spite of it. For Grisaldo there
can be no protracted dalliance; like Samson he would lose
his strength if he were to yield himself to one woman. Thus,
at the end of the first act Grisaldo takes leave of Almerine;
he cannot allow love to hold him back. She begs him to remain, but when at last he yields and is about to sacrifice his
strength and individuality to love, she herself urges him to
go, to keep faith with himself:

Das Weib soll den Helden erhitzen und nicht schwächen. Du
scheidest! Grisaldo, kann die Liebe mit dir von mir scheiden?
Du bist und wirst sein wie meine Liebe. Dieses Herz ist gestärkt
auf ewig in Liebe, so fern du bist.

The premise of Goethe's poem, "Lilis Park," is that the
wild bear must not allow even the most alluring love to de-

base him to the lowly state of a domestic pet:

> Nicht ganz umsonst reck' ich so meine Glieder:
> Ich fühl's! ich schwör's! Noch hab' ich Kraft.

There had been times in his own life when Goethe feared that his attachment to a woman might deprive him of his freedom and leave him an eagle with clipped wings or a giant confined in a small box. Thus in his Sturm-und-Drang period Goethe arrogated to himself the right to sacrifice others, even his own love as well, to his genius. He left Friedericke Brion, as he explains in *Die neue Melusine,* because he dreaded the restrictions of such a relationship; he abandoned Lili because in her social circle he felt like a bear condemned to dance in a parlor. This situation frequently recurs in his writings: a genius must perforce forsake his love if he is to remain true to his inner destiny. The most famous expression of this conflict is to be found in Faust's abandonment of Gretchen. It is Faust's lot to leave Gretchen in misery; for he is like the cataract which must leap from rock to rock, he is the homeless fugitive who may never come to rest. And Gretchen, too, obeys a law higher than the social code; she stifles her conscience when it warns her against yielding completely to passion. She is victimized by Faust and ultimately by society, but in a deeper sense she remains blameless. Although the space devoted to the Gretchen episode, quite apart from its poetic force, would seem to set it in the foreground of the tragedy, it serves dramatically to illustrate only the "Faustian" restlessness, the urge that is never stilled; it is the "episode" of a pebble carried away by a waterfall.

Again, in Goethe's *Stella,* the character Fernando acts on the principle that a man has the right to sacrifice others when his self-fulfillment demands it. On leaving Cäcilie, Fernando had explained to his confidant:[3]

Franz, ich muss fort!—ich wär ein Thor, mich fesseln zu lassen!
Dieser Zustand erstickt alle meine Kräfte, dieser Zustand raubt mir
allen Muth der Seele; er engt mich ein!—Was liegt nicht alles in
mir? Was könnte sich nicht alles entwickeln?—Ich muss fort—in
die freye Welt!—

The play ends with a pleasant "ménage à trois."

Probably the most forthright plea for absolute self-gratification of the individual, especially in affairs of the heart, is
put forward by Heinse in *Ardinghello*. The hero is really a
great man, almost a "superman"; he is accomplished in all
the arts and crafts, is irresistibly attractive to women, and is
outstanding for his passionate nature, his courage, and his
brilliance. After his father is killed because of an illicit affair
with the Duke's daughter, Ardinghello himself is compelled
to flee. For a while he lives with Cäcilia in a veritable frenzy
of passionate enchantment; but upon her marriage he mur-
ders the wealthy bridegroom on the wedding night and is once
more forced to take a hasty departure. He enjoys the em-
braces of Fulvia, a young bride, and all but succeeds in rav-
ishing Lucinde who is herself the child of free love. Lucinde,
who sincerely loves Ardinghello but represses her feelings,
loses her reason. Ardinghello temporarily throws himself into
public life in his native Florence. The first book ends with
the famous description of the Bacchanalia in Rome, in which
young men and women cast off their clothes and abandon
themselves to the dance. The second volume describes Ardinghello's new love affair with Fiordimona. Waylayed and
forced into an affray by a rival who is a relative of the Pope,
the hero kills his opponent and takes refuge with the Grand
Vizier of Turkey, from whom he obtains permission to set
up a utopian state on the isles of Paros and Naxos. Here all
property is communal; the religion is a form of nature worship; the women are emancipated; and sexual promiscuity
is unrestrained. The ethical code of this state not only per-

mits but demands that each individual gratify his desires by any means he finds suitable.

The view that the individual is entitled to complete self-gratification is also basic to Schiller's so-called "Laura" poems, which represent a sensuous vindication of passion. In "Freigeisterei der Leidenschaft" Schiller holds that the solemn vows of matrimony should be broken if they run counter to the individual's natural instincts:

> Weil ein Gebrauch, den die Gesetze heilig prägen,
>   des Zufalls schwere Missetat geweiht?
> Nein—unerschrocken trotz' ich einem Bund entgegen,
>   den die errötende Natur bereut.
>
> O zittre nicht—du hast als Sünderin geschworen,
>   ein Meineid ist der Reue fromme Pflicht.
> Das Herz war mein, das du vor dem Altar verloren,
>   mit Menschenfreuden spielt der Himmel nicht.

He even breaks with a God who demands self-renunciation:

> Besticht man dich mit blutendem Entsagen?
>   Durch eine Hölle nur
> Kannst du zu deinem Himmel Brücken schlagen?
> Nur auf der Folter merkt dich die Natur?

Finally, in his "Resignation," Schiller denounces as a fraud and delusion the hope that self-denial in this world will be compensated in another:

> Was man von der Minute ausgeschlagen,
>   gibt keine Ewigkeit zurück.

SELF-ASSERTION IN THE FACE OF DIVINE AND SOCIAL LAWS

The Stürmer-und-Dränger insist not only on the sexual liberty of the individual, but also upon the abolition of all religious restriction. Particularly do they express a predilection for the hero who maintains his individuality even at the

cost of eternal damnation, as in the original version of *Faust*.
Klinger's Faust actually remains a rebel after death, and his
blasphemy and defiance of divine laws cause Satan himself
to shudder.[4] Again, there is Goethe's "Prometheus," whose
self-assertion goes so far as an onslaught on the Gods themselves.

Family ties and parental influence, too, are mercilessly
attacked by the Sturm-und-Drang. Guelfo, in Klinger's
Zwillinge, defies the father whom he hates. Parents, in many
of the writings of this school, are held to typify the tyranny
of narrow class distinctions and other prejudices which conflict with the rights of children. Thus in Wagner's *Reue nach
der Tat* a mother, seeking at all costs to prevent her son from
marrying a girl of inferior social class, eventually drives the
two lovers to their death. The mother, it is true, suffers
deeply from remorse, but too late. In Schiller's *Kabale und
Liebe* it is the father, bulwarked by the barrier of class, who
stands between the lovers. Here the father represents un-
scrupulous society, with its intrigues, its corruption and its
brutality. Similarly in *Goetz* those who represent society are
weak, deceitful, and faithless; the polished manners, the ob-
sequiousness, and the depravity of the courtier Weislingen
are contrasted with the free, unaffected integrity of Goetz.
Klinger's Faust, on his journey through the world in com-
pany with the Devil, finds debauchery especially among the
upper classes. But Faust, who with the devil's aid assumes
the role of avenger, only aggravates the prevailing injustice.
For society to the Stürmer-und-Dränger is essentially evil
and is not amenable to amelioration.

Klinger's play *Das leidende Weib* depicts the life of an
adulteress who is hunted down by her own conscience as well
as by society. She is a member of an aristocratic family; her
father is a high official of state and her husband an ambas-
sador. They all frequent the court, but they find the atmos-

phere so stultifying that their high rank seems to them a heavy burden. Only by virtually superhuman effort do they manage to remain honest and decent in the service of the court. And it is only at the end of the play, when they have lost both fortune and rank, that these aristocrats find contentment as poor peasants. Thus we see that the Sturm-und-Drang opposes society to a blissful and "natural" life.

Society is held responsible for countless crimes, particularly in the writings of Lenz, who may well be called a pioneer of the "milieu" school. Blame for criminal action is to be charged not to the individual but to society itself. If, as in *Die Soldaten,* the soldiers are driven to a life of debauchery, if a girl turns whore, or if, as in *Der Hofmeister,* a young tutor seduces a maiden, the fault always rests with society. Society enslaves the individual, thwarts his desires, and forces him into crime. Maler Müller even goes so far as to find society guilty of what the Stürmer-und-Dränger tend to regard as the most interesting of crimes—child murder:[5]

Was bracht' sie dazu? Hätte sie das Kind allein in einer Wüste unter wilden Tieren zur Welt bracht, gewiss hätte sie es nicht ermordet. O Menschen, Menschen! Ihr seid ärger als Tiere! Hätte das ganze Dorf nicht mit boshaften Augen das arme Mädchen zuvor so bewacht, allen Schimpf und Schand' vorbereitet, die sie im Fall zu erwarten hatt' . . .: das ist's, was die Natur ganz verdreht, Sanftmut und Liebe in Raserei und Blutdurst verwandelt und das weiche mütterliche Herz eisenfest härtet. Wie in aller Welt wär's denn sonst möglich? Wo kann eine Mutter sein, die ihr Erzeugtes nicht liebet?

To be sure, these accusations are couched for the most part in general terms; they deplore the conflict between individual and society but fail to attack any specific social system.[6] But although the Sturm-und-Drang is far less revolutionary than might today be expected, it must be remembered that such mild criticism appeared in those days as a ferocious onslaught. Only in a few instances is a truly revolutionary tone to be noted: Leisewitz's two dramatic fragments (*Die Pfändung* and *Der Besuch um Mitternacht*), Schubart's writings, and two or three poems in Schiller's "Anthologie" (for example "Die schlimmen Monarchen").

Together with the anti-social individualism of the Sturm-und-Drang, there developed a new patriotism; this was more pronounced in Klopstock and Herder, however, than in the Sturm-und-Drang proper.[7] Nations, too, are in the larger sense individuals, and are thus entitled to free development. Germany above all claims the right to be "German" and to free itself of foreign tutelage, particularly that emanating from France. Nor can the individual attain freedom unless the whole nation, whose condition and character he shares, is also liberated. It must not be supposed, however, that this type of patriotism smacked of chauvinism or intolerance toward other nations; on the contrary, men were now engaged in a sympathetic discovery of other nationalities. Herder, for example, could admire both Greek tragedy and Shakespearean drama. The nation, thus conceived, is not an idol which demands the immolation of its devotees, but rather a congenial world where the free individual may thrive. The patriot, then, is not a nationalist; engaged in the cultivation of his own nature and individuality, he regards the national principle as valid for those in other lands as well.

SUBJECTIVISM IN WERTHER

Although Goethe's *Werther* cannot, strictly speaking, be credited to the Sturm-und-Drang in which the so-called "sentimentalism" has no part, this novel is nevertheless akin to the Sturm-und-Drang in several respects. Werther, like many another hero of this school of literature, is unable to do justice to his abilities. In his case, too, this frustration is caused not by a temporary, curable defect, but by the eternal dissonance between the individual and the world. Werther is subjective, weak, sentimental, not one of those self-assured and forceful characters who would smash up the world if they could. He recoils from society, and suffers when reality invades his dreams. Long before his love for Lotte can reach culmination he makes his escape from the world, "nursing his little heart," and pathologically self-centered. It is not any particular love affair, or any political disappointment, or any unstilled ambition which gives rise to his "Welt-schmerz"; such setbacks serve merely to intensify his profound weariness of man's everlasting limitations.[8] It is this outlook which makes it possible for Werther's love for Lotte to plunge him into despair. At the beginning of the second book, Werther seeks oblivion in work; he is repulsed by society, hurt by its conventions, disgusted by men of affairs. He not only despises the constraints imposed by society, not only hates the all-too-sober normal man, but he claims extraordinary rights, finding only within his being an appropriate measure for his actions. This self-indulgence is particularly evident in his discourse on suicide with Albert: it is the birthright of the exceptional man to be master over his life and death. The individual is a law unto himself.

It is in his egocentricity and his susceptibility to the slights he receives at the hands of society that Werther bears a definite affinity to the Sturm-und-Drang. The difference between *Goetz* and *Werther* is that in *Goetz* the "world" plays an aggressive part in crushing the individual—thus we have a vivid and colorful picture of the world with all its frantic activity—whereas in *Werther* the conflict is viewed through the eyes of the individual—hence the atmosphere of passivity with the colorlessness of the world reflected only in the Ossianic mood of the hero. In *Goetz* we see the destructive forces at work; in *Werther* we witness the agony of the victim.

CHANGES IN THE CONCEPTION OF INDIVIDUALISM

The individualism of the Sturm-und-Drang may be traced in some degree to the Age of Enlightenment and to the proclamation of the Rights of Man. There was a difference, however; for basic to the Rights of Man is the principle that all men are equal, that there is a law common to all which recognizes no distinction of person or class, and to which all men are subject. The Sturm-und-Drang, on the other hand, upholds "the rights of the individual"; since every individual is unique he must have unique rights if he is to attain the freedom he requires. Thus, although the origins of individualism are to be found in the Rights of Man, the conception was developed to such a point that under the influence of Rousseau and the English preromantics, like Edward Young, "originality" and "uniqueness" virtually negated the formulations of the Age of Enlightenment.

By reason of their implicit belief in man's innate sense of justice, the Stürmer-und-Dränger can regard self-assertion as morally just. This sense of justice motivates Goetz, pushing him into conflict with the letter of the law. And only if man acts expressly against this inner sense, as when Franz Moor disregards the loud voice of his conscience, does selfish pursuit of personal profit and pleasure become immoral.

If individualism becomes so extreme that the individual does not recognize any limitations at all, but wants to be and to possess everything, then it develops into virtual negation of individuality. The individual seeks to participate in every human sentiment, to embrace the Infinite. Carrying individualism to its conclusion, he yearns to extend his self until it encompasses the whole of mankind. Individualism has now become insatiable, for the individual seeks both to absorb the universe and to be absorbed by it. Thus the Sturm-und-Drang arrives at a doctrine of pantheistic self-abandonment, an attitude which Goethe expressed in two of his best-known poems. In "Mahomets Gesang" he writes of a mighty river which, constantly impelled by the urge to expand, absorbs all the rivers and streams; yet it remains unsatisfied despite its accretions, and finally rushes on to merge with the ocean:

> Und so trägt er seine Brüder,
> Seine Schätze, seine Kinder,
> Dem erwartenden Erzeuger
> Freudebrausend an das Herz.

And in "Ganymed" the ascension of the hero to Olympus is the symbol of the individual's overflowing into nature and the universe:

> Hinauf! Hinauf strebt's.
> Es schweben die Wolken
> Abwärts, die Wolken
> Neigen sich der sehnenden Liebe.
> Mir! Mir!
> In eurem Schosse
> Aufwärts!
> Umfangend umfangen!
> Aufwärts an deinen Busen,
> Alliebender Vater!

Faust, a typical figure of the Sturm-und-Drang, is forever in revolt against his inability to bring his highest thoughts and ambitions to fruition. The very limitations of his human nature are insufferable to him. He wants to be more than a man, and slumps into utter despair when the Spirit of the Earth points out to him the confines of his being. In particular, Faust is painfully aware of the limits to his knowledge; while Wagner, his complacent famulus, can see no such limits except that time is rather short:

> Ach Gott! die Kunst ist lang;
> Und kurz ist unser Leben . . .

Wie schwer sind nicht die Mittel zu erwerben,
Durch die man zu den Quellen steigt!
Und eh' man nur den halben Weg erreicht,
Muss wohl ein armer Teufel sterben.

But Faust insists that his inability to know everything has nothing to do with time: there is and always will be more beyond his reach than within it. Here too, however, individualism becomes transmuted into a yearning for the Infinite, for something so boundless, so immense, that the individual must become one with the universe if he is to attain it. In the case of Faust also, a broadening of self takes the place of self-assertion.

Thus individualism carried within itself the seed of its own transformation into the classical conception of personality—of the man who is not an individual but a representative of mankind, and in the Faust fragment of 1790 this new tendency is expressed:

Und was der ganzen Menschheit zugeteilt ist,
Will ich in meinem innern Selbst geniessen,
Mit meinem Geist' das Höchst' und Tiefste greifen,
Ihr Wohl und Weh auf meinen Busen häufen,
Und so mein eigen Selbst zu ihrem Selbst erweitern,
Und wie sie selbst, am End' auch ich zerscheitern.

Here is the final and almost paradoxical climax of individualism: the individual seeks to expand to such a point that he may embrace the whole of mankind.

An ever-unstilled urge is the essence of Faust's nature, a curse from which he cannot escape although he craves peace and quietude. Because he knows that his volcanic restlessness will never cease, and because, at the same time, he longs for surcease, he can safely set forth the conditions of his wager with Mephistopheles. At this point is reached the final stage beyond which individualism cannot go.

INDIVIDUALITY IN LITERARY STYLE

We have reviewed the ideas of the Sturm-und-Drang as expressed in the poetry of that school. But here for once we have a palpable connection between the idea and the way in which it is expressed, between content and form. For in their style, too, the Stürmer-und-Dränger strive to express their individuality. They dismiss all laws including the three dramatic unities of time, action and place, as merely arbitrary. They repudiate the traditional laws of versification, of style, and even of grammar, and emphasize instead the original and the spontaneous.

III

CLASSICISM: PERSONALITY AND SOCIETY

GOETHE

GEORG SIMMEL[9] formulated a distinction between two different types of "individuality"—the same two types which Fritz Strich has called "Personality" and "Individuality," and which he has applied in elucidating an important problem in the history of the Renaissance.[10] This distinction has since proved most useful in literary history, especially with reference to the so-called Baroque period.[11]

Personality in this sense means a comprehensive and mature development of character whereby a man, complete within himself, partakes of the whole nature of man. But personality, in Strich's view, does not imply that every man must differ from every other. The ideal of the Renaissance, to be sure, was the realization of the individual's personality, but it was nevertheless possible for every man to conform to the same conventions and laws. Personality is thus markedly different from individuality or singularity.

Individuality, on the other hand, requires the individual to be both quantitatively and qualitatively different from any other, to be unmistakable and unique. Not only must the individual follow an independent existence, but he must be unlike any other individual in substance and quality.

Man achieves personality by giving up everything which is purely individual, by ceasing to be one particular man and becoming a representative of mankind.[12] Whereas individuality is always antagonistic to society, personality can be, and for the classicist actually is, consistent with surrender to society, with self-conquest and self-renunciation. The class-

ical conception of personality includes responsibility, obligation, duty; the conception of Sturm-und-Drang means irre-
sponsibility, freedom, license. To achieve his individuality
the Stürmer must abandon himself to his desires; whereas
the classicist, far from yielding to them, combats the dark
instincts within him. The classicist subordinates himself, of
his own free will, to principles of a higher order than those
of the individual; his personality is based upon self-denial,
self-sacrifice, renunciation—"Entsagung." The highest aim
and, incidentally, the most satisfactory proof that one has
achieved personality is the conquest of one's own self: "Sich
selbst besiegen." The supreme ethical value is performance of
one's duty.

It is the oneness, the completeness, of the Greek which
Goethe in his classical period admires, and the lack of which
he deplores in the modern. Winckelmann, asserts Goethe,
has in a sense arrived at this "Vollständigkeit seiner Persönlichkeit"; and Goethe takes pains to make clear that such
complete personalities have a certain similarity of mind and
attitude. They share a marked degree of harmony and understanding,[13] whereas individuality occupies an inaccessible
world reserved exclusively for a single inhabitant.

It is this distinction between individuality and personality
which constitutes one of the essential differences between
Sturm-und-Drang and classicism. Goethe's famous lines written in 1815:

> Volk and Knecht und Überwinder,
> Sie gestehn zu jeder Zeit:
> Höchstes Glück der Erdenkinder
> Sei nur die Persönlichkeit

would be doubly misunderstood if interpreted as the creed of
an individualist. For in the first place the verse is a reported
statement, and not necessarily subscribed to by Goethe; and
secondly it refers to the classical conception of personality,

not to individuality. Only with such qualification may it be held to summarize Goethe's views.

In the light of the distinctions between individuality and personality it becomes possible to describe more accurately the attitude of both Goethe and Schiller in their classical period toward the French Revolution. They affirm the idea of the Rights of Man, and they approve the French Revolution to the extent that it sought to place equality and freedom within the reach of everyone and thereby to make it possible for all men to be "reine Menschen." But they oppose the Revolution at the point where it released the basest passions of man, so that the individual was no longer content to attain equality with others, and no longer submitted to the common law, but claimed individual freedom. The rights of the "individual," for the very reason that they are different in every case, are incalculable and to a large degree irrational; and it is against this irrationality that Goethe and Schiller turn.

The classical conception, according to which man is only and completely a man and not an individual, finds expression in the characters of classical poetry themselves; the more closely they attain to the ideal of "pure men," the more do they become like one another. Initially they may have been quite different persons—Iphigenie or Thoas, Wilhelm Meister or Lothario—but in the end they may all be called "Humanus," like the old and venerable man in "Die Geheimnisse."

Iphigenie auf Tauris is perhaps as typically classical as any play, and it also serves clearly to illustrate the classical conception of "personality." The central figure is not, as with the Stürmer-und-Dränger, a titan, but an entirely human character, possessing all the ethical qualities which render man worthy to be so called. *Iphigenie* does not extol self-indulgence and self-gratification; it glorifies moderation, renunciation and humanity. The characters here are not essentially different from one another; they have in common certain qualities and are united by a common human bond. Furthermore they all move toward the same ideal, and their differences reflect only their varying stages of development with reference to it. Not by their individuality, but by their assimilation to one and the same standard, do the characters attain to the ideal of personality.

Iphigenie dwells in the land of the Taurians as priestess to Diana. She has taught the Taurians humanity and brought them prosperity; but when she refuses an offer of marriage from King Thoas, he threatens to restore the rite of human sacrifice. The first two sacrificial victims are to be Orestes and his friend Pylades who have been sent to Tauris (as Goethe calls it) by Apollo to "recover the sister" and thereby to expiate the matricide of which Orestes is guilty. They believe that Apollo's command refers to the image of Diana, Apollo's sister. In Euripides' drama they capture the image by cunning and deceit. But Goethe, by making the god's command refer to Orestes' sister Iphigenie, dispenses with the necessity of deceit; with him it is truth and morality which serve as talismans of success. Goethe's Orestes confesses his identity because he cannot permit the priestess to be deceived; and she, in turn, confesses the plot to the king and places their lives in his hands. The very humanity of the characters, their generosity, and not least their self-renunciation, serve to bring about the conciliatory end: Thoas especially achieves complete personality by giving up his love, and thus at last attains equality with Iphigenie, who throughout had been his teacher and guide. Iphigenie opens the play with a monologue in which she expresses her longing for her native country and describes the resignation and renunciation required by her sacred office. From early youth Iphigenie has learned to serve, and in serving she feels most free:

Von Jugend auf hab' ich gelernt gehorchen,
Erst meinen Eltern und dann einer Gottheit,
Und folgsam fühlt' ich immer meine Seele
Am schönsten frei.   (V, 3)

Personality, since it does not involve individual self-assertion, need not come into conflict with society. Indeed the moral obligations of the characters in *Iphigenie* toward one another, and their personal adjustments in this respect, may be regarded as "social" proprieties in a deeper sense.

In *Tasso*, a companion play to *Iphigenie*, the theme is the open conflict between the individual and society. But whereas in the Sturm-und-Drang the right lay always and invariably with the individual, the situation is now reversed. Tasso, the poet, the genius who stands for individuality, is in the wrong. When he advocates subjectivity as a law unto itself, in the famous pronouncement: "Erlaubt ist, was gefällt," he is at once reprimanded by the Princess, who replies: "Erlaubt ist, was sich ziemt." The play is set in the court of Alfons, Duke of Ferrara; here we have a "seat of the Muses," but nonetheless a center of polished and refined manners in which moral obligation and social adjustment are stressed. Just as Tasso represents individuality, so Antonio, the man of affairs, stands for all the proprieties. Again and again Tasso fails to achieve reconciliation with the statesman Antonio, or, in a broader sense, to find his way into society, to respect the manners of the court, to learn to become less subjective, less individualistic, less self-assertive. In spite of good will and friendly assistance, Tasso blindly misses his way, but the reader is always kept aware that this failure indicates a serious defect in Tasso himself. The ideal which now motivates and guides is self-restraint, or conformity with the requirements of society.

Tasso is perhaps the best illustration of what is meant by

the "inevitability" of the conflict. It is no one particular society, conditioned by time or place or other factors, which clashes with the individual, but society itself; hence the conflict becomes inevitable, tragic in the deepest sense. As long as society remains society, and the individual remains an individual, no solution is possible. For reconciliation with society requires heroic, self-sacrificial renunciation on the part of the individual, and it is here precisely that Tasso is found wanting.

Tasso, as we have seen, illustrates the difference between Sturm-und-Drang and classicism. And it is interesting to recall that Goethe himself had to make the sacrifice he demands of Tasso, had to turn from self-gratification to self-restraint when he took up his duties and responsibilities as Minister in Weimar.

Before Goethe left for Weimar, he wrote his poem "Adler und Taube." Here, an eagle, badly injured, loses the use of his wings, and a dove attempts to console him with a picture of the pleasures and comforts to be enjoyed on the ground. The eagle, however, cannot share the dove's contentment although he envies him his happiness. This is another instance of the "Faustian" conflict: yearning in vain for the Infinite, the hero yet longs with all his heart for a single moment of rest and peace. But in 1781, in "Grenzen der Menschheit," Goethe accepts the very limitation against which he had formerly rebelled. And two years later, in 1783, in a birthday poem for the Duke, "Ilmenau," he accuses himself of having unwisely advocated unrestrained pride and liberty:

> Und wenn ich unklug Mut und Freiheit sang
> Und Redlichkeit und Freiheit sonder Zwang,
> Stolz auf sich selbst und herzliches Behagen,
> Erwarb ich mir der Menschen schöne Gunst;
> Doch ach! ein Gott versagte mir die Kunst,
> Die arme Kunst mich künstlich zu betragen.

The eagle has bowed his head in heroic renunciation. Goethe now depicts the pleasures of a peaceful, modest, and industrious people. Urging submission and renunciation, Goethe admonishes the Duke to forego his own desires and to concentrate upon serving others:

> Ich sehe hier wie man nach langer Reise
> Im Vaterland sich wieder kennt,
> Ein ruhig Volk im stillen Fleisse
> Benutzen, was Natur an Gaben ihm gegönnt.
> Der Faden eilet von dem Rocken
> Des Webers raschem Stuhle zu;
> Und Seil und Kübel wird in längrer Ruh
> Nicht am verbrochnen Schachte stocken;
> Es wird der Trug entdeckt, die Ordnung kehrt zurück,
> Es folgt Gedeihn und festes irdsches Glück.

> So mög', o Fürst, der Winkel deines Landes
> Ein Vorbild deiner Tage sein!
> Du kennest lang die Pflichten deines Standes
> Und schränkest nach und nach die freie Seele ein.
> Der kann sich manchen Wunsch gewähren,
> Der kalt sich selbst und seinem Wunsche lebt;
> Allein wer andre wohl zu leiten strebt,
> Muss fähig sein, viel zu entbehren.

Some ten years later (1796–97), Goethe wrote *Hermann und Dorothea,* his classical poem in praise of "Bürgertum"; here he extols civic order, modesty, simplicity, contented self-control, burgeois order and prosperity. At first glance this poem appears to stress a theme characteristic of the Sturm-und-Drang: the father objects to the marriage of his son because he considers it a "mésalliance." But there similarity ends: the son does not defy his father; instead he recognizes the fact that his father is right.[14] Can one imagine Ferdinand, in *Kabale und Liebe,* insisting to his father that Luise, after all, is just as good a match as Lady Milford? The bourgeois, domestic virtues are now of prime importance, and the bride-to-be must offer either a large dowry or a "potential" dowry in that she is equipped to manage household affairs as a thrifty and dutiful wife. The limited, simple, industrious life of the "Bürger" is glorified without apology in this "Idyll." It is interesting, however, to note the difference between the simple life which is stressed here and which is the product of conscious social adaptation and self-abnegation and the simple patriarchal life which Rousseau and the Stürmer-und-Dränger idealized as opposed to the unnatural life of "society."

Goethe's conviction that salvation lies in self-limitation grows stronger with his classicism; the idea of "Entsagung" begins to dominate his thought and poetry.[15] Thus, under the influence of Frau von Stein, Goethe in 1784–85 composes "Die Geheimnisse" in which the saintly Master of a religious Order—significantly called "Humanus"—achieves the perfection of his personality. He is not an individual; he is not "a" man but "the" man. Having learned obedience and service as a boy, he has triumphantly emerged from the most difficult ordeal of self-conquest.

> Doch wenn ein Mann von allen Lebensproben
> Die sauerste besteht, sich selbst bezwingt,
> Dann kann man ihn mit Freuden andern zeigen
> Und sagen: Das ist er, das ist sein eigen.
>
> Denn alle Kraft dringt vorwärts in die Weite,
> Zu leben und zu wirken hier und dort;
> Dagegen engt und hemmt von jeder Seite
> Der Strom der Welt und reisst uns mit sich fort.
> In diesem innern Sturm und äussern Streite
> Vernimmt der Geist ein schwer verstanden Wort:
> Von der Gewalt, die alle Wesen bindet,
> Befreit der Mensch sich, der sich überwindet.

In Goethe's prologue, *Was wir bringen* (1802), we find the well known sonnet "Natur und Kunst, sie scheinen sich zu fliehen." And although the lines here quoted refer primarily to Goethe's aesthetic views, they represent equally well his ethical and social ideal.

So ist's mit aller Bildung auch beschaffen,
Vergebens werden ungebundne Geister
Nach der Vollendung reiner Höhe streben.

Wer Grosses will, muss sich zusammenraffen.
In der Beschränkung zeigt sich erst der Meister,
Und das Gesetz nur kann uns Freiheit geben.

Again the connection between content and form is apparent; for in their style, too, the classicists aim at objectivity, perfection, and conformity to immutable laws.

This insistence on law and order, on the subordination of the individual, so strikingly opposed to the individualism of Sturm-und-Drang, Goethe expresses in a much-quoted sentence, whose meaning has been distorted to justify political oppression and injustice. Thus, in *Die Belagerung von Mainz*,[16] Goethe goes so far as to say, "Es liegt nun einmal in meiner Natur: ich will lieber eine Ungerechtigkeit begehen, als Unordnung ertragen." Perhaps he might more correctly have stated, not that he naturally preferred injustice to disorder, but that this was the ideal to which self-discipline and renunciation had brought him.

From *Clavigo* to the final scenes of the second part of *Faust*, from the play penned when he was turning from Sturm-und-Drang to classicism to virtually the last lines he ever wrote, there is an unbroken sequence of "Entsagungsdichtung." This tendency is clearly to be noted, particularly in his outstanding works: *Clavigo, Wilhelm Meister, Wahlverwandtschaften, Die natürliche Tochter* and *Faust*.

Clavigo once more treats a subject common to the Sturm-und-Drang, and again stresses an ideal which stands in contradiction to that of the earlier school. An ambitious man who has climbed almost to the pinnacle of success is halted by his obligation to a woman. His friend, Carlos, an advocate of the Sturm-und-Drang point of view, persuades Clavigo to sacrifice Marie to his ambitions. He urges the fulfillment of the exceptional man and inveighs against complacency and restrictive domesticity:[17]

Sich häuslich niederlassen, sich einschränken, da man noch die Hälfte seiner Wanderung nicht zurückgelegt, die Hälfte seiner Eroberungen noch nicht gemacht hat!

Carlos encourages Clavigo to pursue his ambition, to make the best use of his resources and to escape the restraints which Marie would impose upon him.[18]

Aber auch da, Clavigo, sei ein ganzer Kerl und mache deinen Weg stracks, ohne rechts und links zu sehen. Möge deine Seele sich erweitern und die Gewissheit des grossen Gefühls über dich kommen, dass ausserordentliche Menschen eben auch darin ausserordentliche Menschen sind, weil ihre Pflichten von den Pflichten des gemeinen Menschen abgehen; dass der, dessen Werk es ist, ein grosses Ganze zu übersehen, zu regieren, zu erhalten, sich keinen Vorwurf zu machen braucht, geringe Verhältnisse vernachlässiget, Kleinigkeiten dem Wohl des Ganzen aufgeopfert zu haben. Tut das der Schöpfer in seiner Natur, der König in seinem Staate— warum sollten wir's nicht tun, um ihnen ähnlich zu werden?

This is indeed a sermon in the Sturm-und-Drang tradition. But Carlos does not represent Goethe's views. Sincere he may be, but his teachings are false. He is a seducer and his influence is evil. For man never has the right to sacrifice the life and happiness of others to his genius; duty makes certain demands which man cannot deny. The theme here is classical restraint, which governs not only the tenor of the play but, for the first time with Goethe, also the style.

We have already seen how *Iphigenie* and *Tasso* extol not individuality but personality based on self-restraint and social adaptation. In the classical period of German literature there is also a new interpretation of the role of Woman. Frau von Stein in Goethe's own life, Iphigenie, the Princess in *Tasso,* and Helena in *Faust* all represent society and propriety; they serve as the educative force which turns individualists into responsible members of society. Here again there is a remarkable contrast to the Stürmer-und-Dränger, whose women were either self-assertive like the men or victims of the male's drive for self-expression. And it is significant that in *Wilhelm Meister,* Goethe's great "novel of development," women play a decisive part in the hero's education. He concludes his apprenticeship when he meets Natalie, an active worker in a limited sphere; for Wilhelm proceeds from individualism to society, from self-assertion to self-renunciation.

What is the content of *Wilhelm Meister* if we look at the novel in its final form, neglecting for the moment the history of its creation? Wilhelm finds himself utterly dissatisfied with the bourgeois atmosphere of his father's home. Although it must be admitted that he is not essentially a Faustian character whose feeling of frustration shatters his world, it is true nevertheless that Wilhelm bears some affinity to both Faust and Werther. He, too, seeks self-realization and encounters external resistance. He is drawn to the theater; but the theater seems only an arbitrary choice, for Wilhelm is certainly as much a poet as an actor. What he really desires is the life of the artist. He looks upon the artist not as a man who works earnestly and tirelessly, subjecting himself to severe discipline, but as one who leads a life of perfect liberty. Disappointed in his great love for an actress, Wilhelm undertakes a business trip and sets out on a series of journeys. He joins a group of actors, he stays at a baronial castle, meets and makes friends with men and women of all types. Thus in the "Lehrjahre" the world and society do not stand for frustration as they did in "Werther"; they are

"Bildungsmächte," educational forces which shape, mature, and perfect the hero.

Most important for Wilhelm is his contact with the members of the "Society of the Tower," a group which had guided him from the beginning and now receives him into its midst. Here he finds busy, active and practical men who take upon themselves a multitude of duties and tasks. Likewise he meets Therese, the "bonne menagère," the active woman, profoundly resourceful, who with unfailing devotion and altruism conducts the affairs of the household and looks to the comfort of its inmates. From his longing for self-fulfillment he is now awakened to an appreciation of self-denial and service. The same Wilhelm who once fled from the drudgery and dullness of his father's business can say that he is about to associate with men who will inevitably show him the way to definite and suitable activity:[19]

Ich verlasse das Theater und verbinde mich mit Männern, deren Umgang mich in jedem Sinne zu einer reinen und sicheren Tätigkeit führen muss.

He knows now that the individual must forget himself in activity prescribed by duty, must submerge his ego in the mass of men, and finally learn to live for the sake of others:[20]

dann ist es vorteilhaft, wenn er sich in einer grösseren Masse verlieren lernt, wenn er lernt, um anderer willen zu leben und seiner selbst in einer pflichtmässigen Tätigkeit zu vergessen.

The culmination of his new tendency to renunciation is reached when Wilhelm finds his son and undertakes to carry out the duties and responsibilities of fatherhood.

Wilhelm Meisters Lehrjahre traces one man's development from individualism to self-renunciation and social service. Wilhelm does not achieve unique individuality; rather he strives for equality with the most perfect personality—Natalie—who from early youth has lived for others. She has never been susceptible to the charms of nature or of art but has always sought to be of service:[21]

Die Reize der leblosen Natur, für die so viele Menschen äusserst empfänglich sind, hatten keine Wirkung auf mich, beinah noch weniger die Reize der Kunst; meine angenehmste Empfindung war und ist es noch, wenn sich mir ein Mangel, ein Bedürfnis in der Welt darstellte, sogleich im Geiste einen Ersatz, ein Mittel, eine Hilfe aufzufinden.

And Natalie explicitly rejects individual liberty and self-indulgence, holding that it is better to err with method than to follow one's own inclination. An unequivocal law is almost a good in itself:[22]

Ja, ich möchte beinah behaupten: es sei besser nach Regeln zu irren, als zu irren, wenn uns die Willkür unserer Natur hin und her treibt; und wie ich die Menschen sehe, scheint mir in ihrer Natur immer eine Lücke zu bleiben, die nur durch ein entschieden aus-gesprochenes Gesetz ausgefüllt werden kann.

It must be remembered that Natalie serves to a large extent as a mouthpiece through which the moral of the novel is expressed.

Natalie also stands for what might almost be called a new religion: "Weltfrömmigkeit." Social work and good deeds are more important than prayers and faith. Natalie keeps both feet firmly on the ground, and Wilhelm too comes down to earth and learns to devote his services to the world of here and now.

This type of education and indeed Wilhelm's ultimate conversion had been suggested to him earlier by the memoirs of the "schöne Seele" with which he had become acquainted before he joined the "Society of the Tower."

Phyllis, the fair saint, or as Goethe calls her, "die schöne Seele," writes that she has found consolation and comfort for her poor health in piety. Without worldly ambition, she has concentrated upon the salvation of her soul. Her uncle, how-

ever, insists that to cultivate one's own soul is merely a refined form of selfishness and lectures her on the necessity of
an active life:[23]

Das ganze Weltwesen liegt vor uns wie ein grosser Steinbruch vor
dem Baumeister, der nur dann den Namen verdient, wenn er aus
diesen zufälligen Naturmassen ein in seinem Geiste entsprungenes
Urbild mit der grössten Ökonomie, Zweckmässigkeit and Festig-
keit zusammenstellt. Alles ausser uns ist nur Element, ja ich darf
wohl sagen auch alles an uns; aber tief in uns liegt diese schöp-
ferische Kraft, die das zu erschaffen vermag, was sein soll, und
uns nicht ruhen und rasten lässt, bis wir es ausser uns oder an uns,
auf eine oder die andere Weise, dargestellt haben. Sie, liebe Nichte,
haben vielleicht das beste Teil erwählt; Sie haben Ihr sittliches
Wesen, Ihre tiefe liebevolle Natur mit sich selbst und mit dem
höchsten Wesen übereinstimmend zu machen gesucht, indes wir
andern wohl auch nicht zu tadeln sind, wenn wir den sinnlichen
Menschen in seinem Umfang zu kennen und tätig in Einheit zu
bringen suchen.

Phyllis' uncle not only rejects passivity and "Weltflucht,"
but recommends self-limitation as a means to efficiency. Man
should have some sphere of purposeful and determinate activity:[24]

Der Mensch ist zu einer beschränkten Lage geboren; einfache,
nahe, bestimmte Zwecke vermag er einzusehen, und er gewöhnt
sich die Mittel zu benutzen, die ihm gleich zur Hand sind; sobald
er aber ins Weite kommt, weiss er weder, was er will, noch was er
soll, und es ist ganz einerlei, ob er durch die Menge der Gegenstände
zerstreut, oder ob er durch die Höhe und Würde derselben ausser
sich gesetzt werde. Es ist immer ein Unglück, wenn er veranlasst
wird, nach etwas zu streben, mit dem er sich durch eine regel-
mässige Selbsttätigkeit nicht verbinden kann.

The ideal is not Phyllis, but Natalie; not the inactive, in-
trospective "saint," but the forceful, energetic worker in the
everyday world. Precision and perseverance are the supreme
desiderata, and man should follow the dictates of duty, not
of pleasure, or even of circumstances.

To be a useful member of society, to subordinate oneself
to the law, to impose some limitation upon oneself—how
different are these precepts from those of the Sturm-und-
Drang! [25] Indeed they contrast sharply not only with
Werther's ideals but also with Grimmelshausen's *Simplicissimus*, the "Bildungsroman" of the seventeenth century.
Simplicissimus, too, is educated in and by the world; but the
world can teach him only the futility and vanity of earthly
existence. Life in this world is shown to be completely without purpose except as preparation for the world-to-come.
Simplicissimus starts out on his adventures from a hermit's
hut only to return to a hermit's hut at the end. In the sixth
book, added to the work at a later date, Simplicissimus leaves
the hermit's hut once more, but after a few additional adventures he retires to a desert island, confirmed in his belief that
only the Kingdom of God has reality and that all worldly
affairs are vain.

Wilhelm Meister learns, during his apprenticeship, self-
limitation, subordination to the norm, and the value of useful, competent work in the everyday world. When he has
learned this much and, for the first time in his life, has taken
on important responsibilities, he is presented with his "in-
denture," a summary of the new wisdom he has acquired.
Every faculty, every art, every capacity, he is told, lies in
man—not in the one but in the many. Gifts are distributed
among men, and each man should cultivate his own alone.
"It is all men who constitute mankind; all powers taken
together make up the world":[26] ("Nur alle Menschen machen
die Menschheit aus, nur alle Kräfte zusammengenommen die
Welt").

A "man is never happy until his vague striving has itself
marked out its proper limitations":[27] ("Der Mensch ist nicht
eher glücklich, als bis sein unbedingtes Streben sich selbst
seine Grenzen bestimmt"). It is this maxim which is basic to

the *Wanderjahre*, with all its digressions and elaborations.
When Wilhelm set out on his quest for self-fulfillment, he
wrote the famous letter to Werner attacking "burgher" complacency and narrowness. Since the burgher, if he is to be a
useful citizen, must cultivate one single gift at the expense
of all others, it is clear that there can be no harmony in his
life:[28]

Er (der Bürger) soll einzelne Fähigkeiten ausbilden, um brauchbar zu werden, und es wird schon vorausgesetzt, dass in seinem
Wesen keine Harmonie sei, noch sein dürfe, weil er, um sich auf
eine Weise brauchbar zu machen, alles übrige vernachlässigen muss.

Ultimately, however, Wilhelm himself subscribes to the very
limitation which he disparages in this letter. Already when
he finds his son, Wilhelm is said to have acquired all the
virtues of the "burgher" with the emotions of paternity.
And at the close of his travels, he takes up one definite,
limited, useful profession, surgery, and becomes a member of
the society which calls itself "Das Band." By self-denial
and self-renunciation, by making the most difficult and heroic
sacrifice of his individuality, by subordinating himself to
society, Wilhelm finally attains to "personality."

The sub-title of the *Travels* expresses Goethe's ideal:
"Die Entsagenden." Wilhelm, while journeying, meets many
people who teach him renunciation: Makarie who educates,
assists, advises; Nachodine, the "Schöne-Gute," another
woman of vision, determination, and activity like Natalie;
the "Oheim"; and many others. Again and again, the importance of self-restraint and of a useful activity within
society is brought home to Wilhelm, notably by the methods
of the "pedagogical province" where his son is educated to
a definite occupation, that of horse groom.

Jarno-Montan, one of the major characters, insists on the
superiority of handicraft and of the man who, by manual
effort, produces some useful commodity:[29]

Ja, es ist jetzo die Zeit der Einseitigkeiten; wohl dem, der es begreift, für sich und andere in diesem Sinne wirkt. Bei gewissen Dingen versteht's sich durchaus und sogleich. Übe dich zum tüchtigen Violinisten und sei versichert, der Kapellmeister wird dir deinen Platz im Orchester mit Gunst anweisen. Mache ein Organ aus dir und erwarte, was für eine Stelle dir die Menschheit im allgemeinen Leben wohlmeinend zugestehen wird. Lass uns abbrechen! Wer es nicht glauben will, der gehe seinen Weg, auch der gelingt zuweilen; ich aber sage: von unten hinauf zu dienen, ist überall nötig. Sich auf ein Handwerk zu beschränken, ist das Beste. Für den geringsten Kopf wird es immer ein Handwerk, für den besseren eine Kunst, und der beste, wenn er Eins tut, tut er alles, oder um weniger parodox zu sein, in dem einen, was er recht tut, sieht er das Gleichnis von allem, was recht getan wird.

A similar view is expressed by the antiquarian from whom Wilhelm seeks advice about the education of his son:[30]

Allem Leben, allem Tun, aller Kunst muss das Handwerk vorausgehen, welches nur in der Beschränkung erworben wird. Eines recht wissen und ausüben, gibt höhere Bildung als Halbheit im Hundertfältigen.

If Goethe eulogizes the craftsman, he means the sober, practical, skilled manual worker, in contrast to the picturesque, "romanticized," essentially artistic figure whom he himself had described in his poem "Hans Sachsens poetische Sendung" and whom the romanticists were later to idealize as continuing the tradition of the medieval craftsman.[31] So Wilhelm, who began as an individualist and artist, ends as a skilled surgeon, a χειρουργικος, a manual worker, whose dexterity makes him a useful member of society. The virtues of the "Bürger," derided at first, are at last almost sanctified: the citizen becomes a "super-citizen."

What actual form the society envisaged in *Die Wanderjahre* was to take remains a matter of doubt. Goethe was engaged in writing a novel, and not a sociological treatise. There is, to be sure, a difference between the system of the

"Oheim" and the constitution contemplated by the "Band";
and it is significant that some of the travelers remain in
Germany and adapt themselves to the existing monarchy,
while others emigrate to the virgin soil of America. But it
can safely be assumed, however, that whatever the details,
Goethe's society exerts authority over the individual and
makes exacting demands upon him. It is clear, moreover,
that this society will not satisfy the wants and desires of the
individual.[32]

During this phase of his development Goethe suggests that
every man should take up some useful activity which might
divert his attention from political issues:[33]

Was mich betrifft, so sehe ich nur immer mehr ein, dass jeder nur
sein Handwerk ernsthaft treiben und das Übrige alles lustig
nehmen soll. Ein paar Verse, die ich zu machen habe, interessieren
mich jetzt mehr als viel wichtigere Dinge, auf die mir kein Einfluss
gestattet ist, und wenn ein jeder das Gleiche tut, so wird es in der
Stadt und im Hause wohl stehen.

And in almost identical terms Goethe presents this view in
the epigram "Bürgerpflicht" ("Ein jeder kehre vor seiner
Tür . . ."). The title itself is significant: "civic duty." To
follow his vocation, to do his duty, and therein to find contentment—this is the virtue of the "Bürger." We have
already observed this ideal in *Hermann und Dorothea* and
in the poem "Ilmenau," in which is described the idyllic
tranquillity resulting from such a contented and limited existence. We have also noted Wilhelm Meister's conversion to
a bourgeois life. In *Der Bürgergeneral,* one of the earlier
plays in which Goethe tackles the problem of the French
Revolution, the nobleman in his final speech warns the aged
Märten to mind his own business and to regard the constel-
lation of the political firmament, if at all, on festal days only.
(It is true that the nobleman at the same time inveighs
against the iniquity of his peers, which he holds responsible

for the unrest among the commons.) At a time when politics and affairs of state loomed large in the minds of most Germans, Goethe in his *Vorspiel zur Eröffnung des Weimarischen Theaters* (1807) praises the complacent domesticity, the useful activity, the fulfillment of civic duty, indeed the very limitations which he believes will ensure political stability:

> Wer das Rechte will, der sollt es können,
> Und ein jeder kanns, der sich bescheidet,
> Schöpfer seines Glücks zu sein im Kleinen . . .
>
> Es lohnt sich
> Jeder selbst, der sich im stillen Hausraum
> Wohl befleissigt übernommenen Tagwerks,
> Freudig das Begonnene vollendet.

A similar laudatory treatment of activity, but without the "bourgeois" strain, is to be found in *Pandora*. Prometheus, who, to the youthful Goethe, represented the essence of soaring titanism, is now the practical man of action. His brother Epimetheus symbolizes the other extreme, the "vita contemplativa." It was probably the poet's intention that *Pandora* should illustrate the synthesis of these two extremes: action guided by thought, beauty realized in productive creation.

Interspersed in *Die Wanderjahre* are a series of short stories, most of them in one way or another "Entsagungsnovellen." And most of Goethe's "Novellen," including that actually called *Novelle*, as well as the exempla, anecdotes and stories from the *Unterhaltungen*, preach the same lesson of self-renunciation, of the supremacy of civic society. One story, originally intended for the *Wanderjahre*, but later developed into a full-length novel, may well serve as an example of the many. This is *Die Wahlverwandtschaften*, perhaps Goethe's most deliberately planned work.

The action of this novel takes place on the large estate of a wealthy baron. The baron, Eduard, wishes to invite an army captain, his best friend, to his home. Charlotte, the baron's wife, raises grave objections. She and Eduard had long been in love, had endured a separation, and were now enjoying a happy union. Because she fears any possible intrusion, she wishes to exclude from Eduard's home her niece Ottilie as well. Eventually, however, Eduard has his way, and both Ottilie and the captain arrive as guests. Soon Eduard and Ottilie on the one hand, and Charlotte and the captain on the other, fall victims to sexual attraction. The marriage between Eduard and Charlotte is seriously threatened and indeed they indulge in a sort of spiritual adultery; for Charlotte, in the arms of Eduard, now thinks of the captain, and Eduard in the arms of Charlotte, longs for Ottilie. Marriage has become an almost insupportable burden to this once-happy couple. The captain leaves. Charlotte, not without struggle, renounces her love for him and in the hope of restoring the former relationship, plans to send Ottilie away. But Eduard cannot bring himself to the point of parting with Ottilie, whom he loves with a passion which amounts almost to madness. This love conditions not only his happiness but his very life. Having refused to renounce Ottilie, he goes off to war, where he seeks death on the battlefield.

At this point, the protagonists are relegated to the background of the novel while new characters come to the fore: the architect; Charlotte's daughter Luciane, a bustling, whirlwind character; and the "pedagogical assistant" from Ottilie's former school. Thus months go by, until the birth of Charlotte's son, who appears to resemble both Ottilie and the captain. Even now Eduard cannot be persuaded to return to his wife; he is still gripped by his love for Ottilie. She, however, resolves to "renounce" Eduard. While seeking to obtain a divorce from Charlotte, Eduard by chance meets Ottilie and pleads with her when she is taking Charlotte's child out for an airing; agitated by this interview, Ottilie hurries back with the child, crossing the lake in a small boat. The boat is upset and the child is drowned in spite of Ottilie's desperate efforts. Ottilie's sorrow is all the deeper because she sees in this accident a portent of her guilt; she has in spirit violated the law. Now her mind is made up and she is determined never to see Eduard again. Nevertheless, against her will and also against Eduard's, she is to see him again; it seems impossible for her to escape her destiny. She returns to his home, outwardly calm and happy, but actually practicing the most severe self-castigation. She can never cease to love Eduard; they are still attracted to each other irresistibly. But Ottilie does not speak, and slowly starves herself to death; on Eduard's birthday she finally succumbs. And her body, like the relic of a saint, works miracles after death.

There can be no doubt as to the intent of this novel; it represents the sanctification and glorification of self-sacrifice even when carried to the extreme of physical self-destruction. The sacrifice is all the greater and ethically the more valuable because it is almost superhumanly difficult; and subordination to the institution of marriage is the more praiseworthy precisely because its exigencies have proved so burdensome. Remembering the ardent plea of the Stürmer-und-Dränger for unrestricted self-assertion in love, remembering Goethe's own *Werther,* and anticipating the romantic doctrine that marriage without love is worse than crime, we can appreciate the significance of Goethe's classical position.

Goethe was not the first German poet to treat the problem of marriage in a novel. Jean Paul describes in *Siebenkäs* the marriage of a man of literary and scholarly tastes to a good but rather Philistine wife, whose clanging of pots and scratching of brooms torment his nerves and distract him from his work. Eventually Siebenkäs stages his own death and funeral

and disappears to find happiness with another woman, leaving his wife to marry a man more congenial to her tastes.
This is the Sturm-und-Drang conception: Siebenkäs is actually morally obligated to take any steps necessary to the
full development of his "genius." It is particularly interesting
to compare Jean Paul's "lax" views on marriage with Goethe's
"Entsagung," which is achieved only after desperate inward
struggle.

For Goethe marriage is really a "social" problem. He cites
the sixth commandment only to turn it from a religious precept into a social maxim. Marriage is the fountainhead of
social order and tranquility; the family is the pillar of the
state, and all culture derives from the institution of marriage.
Parents must stay together for the sake of their children.

But apart from the central problem of marriage, there is
apparent throughout the novel a definite tendency to subordinate the individual to super-individual laws. The characters themselves are types rather than distinct persons. They
have a function but no individuality; they are even labeled
as representatives of entire classes or professions: the architect, the pedagogical assistant, the captain. The novel tends
to be a typical and general "exemplum," not the record of an
individual case. Generalizations and sententious, abstract
formulae recur constantly. Thus the ideas and the content of
the novel as well as its style and form are conditioned by the
fundamental subordination of the individual to the general
abstract law.

The characters are neither inactive, sentimental dreamers
like the introvert Werther, nor titanic heroes for whose activity even the whole universe is too small; they are in a
sense utilitarians, applying their energy to a definitely limited
field. All are useful workers—gardeners and agriculturists,
chemists and physicists, architects and surgeons, social
workers and administrators. Like Goethe in this period, they

apply their energy to practical tasks. And in their social en-
terprises they stand for organization and large-scale planning,
not for individual initiative and piecemeal execution. The
individual ought to dovetail into the new, comprehensive
order. Thus Eduard and the captain reconstruct on a comprehensive scheme an entire village where formerly each
individual had built his own home and protected it as he
thought best. Goethe here does not look to democratic coöperation of free individuals for social improvement, but to
authority and subordination: "Alles eigentlich gemeinsame
Gute muss durch das unumschränkte Majestätsrecht geför-
dert werden." The pedagogical assistant advocates a stand-
ardized non-individual existence and even the wearing of
uniforms so that the individual shall merge with the mass:[34]

Männer sollten von Jugend auf Uniform tragen, weil sie sich
gewöhnen müssen zusammen zu handeln, sich unter ihresgleichen
zu verlieren, in Masse zu gehorchen und ins Ganze zu arbeiten.

In 1805, just before he became interested in the plan of
Die Wahlverwandtschaften, Goethe rewrote Stella. We have
already discussed the Sturm-und-Drang version, in which
Fernando claimed the right to free himself of any ties which
might interfere with the realization of his individuality.
The original play, it will be recalled, ended with a "ménage
à trois." This denouement, it has been said, was to serve only
as a makeshift until such time as Goethe could find a better
one; but it was consistent with other Sturm-und-Drang
works, as for example Lenz's Die Freunde machen den
Philosophen, a play with a similar ending (here the husband
cedes his wife to her lover). Whether Goethe considered the
conclusion temporary or not, he revised the play in 1805,
eliminating the passage quoted above in which Fernando
claims the birthright of the exceptional man, and altering the
final scene so as to uphold the sanctity of marriage. These

two versions of the same play serve to illustrate the transition from individualism to the principle that individual freedom should bow to the dictates of society.[35]

At about the same time, Goethe planned a great trilogy which was to have embodied his views on the French Revolution. Only the first part, *Die natürliche Tochter* was finished (1802). But even as it stands, this drama is another example of "Entsagungsdichtung." The heroine, Eugenie, is the natural daughter of a duke who, at the opening of the play, requests the king to grant her legitimate status because of her noble parentage. But a group of intriguing politicians, fearing that she might interfere with their schemes, carry her off and demand that she choose between banishment to an island so fever-ridden that it promises an early death, or marriage to a burgher. She can remain safe if she renounces her birthright and settles down as an ordinary citizen:

> Den werten Zögling wünscht' ich lange schon
> Vom Glück zu überzeugen, das im Kreise
> Des Bürgerstandes hold genügsam weilt.
> Entsagte sie der nicht gegönnten Höhe,
> Ergäbe sich des biedern Gatten Schutz
> Und wendete von jenen Regionen,
> Wo sie Gefahr, Verbannung, Tod umlauern,
> Ins Häusliche den liebevollen Blick:
> Gelöst wär' alles . . .
>
> (IV, 1)

Eugenie is impetuous, willful and foolhardy. For example, at a hunt she once stubbornly and daringly plunged down a declivity and nearly broke her neck. And at the prospect of entering into her noble estate, she evinced such overweening pride that even her father became uneasy. She went so far as to violate his express command and disregarded the repeated warnings of her governess when she flaunted her princely gowns and jewels.

It is obvious, then, that Eugenie must consider it unbearable to renounce her rights:

> Ich könnte die Geburt,
> Die mich so hoch hinaufgerückt, verleugnen!
> Von allem Glanze jener Hoffnung mich
> Auf ewig trennen! Das vermag ich nicht!
>
> (V, 6)

Nevertheless, when a monk informs her that political upheaval threatens her country, she decides to forego her title, marry a burgher and sacrifice her social ambition in order to remain and support her native land. She even asks the man she is about to marry whether he is willing to renounce love and to share in her sacrifice:

> Vermagst du, hohen Muts,
> Entsagung der Entsagenden zu weihen?
>
> (V, 9)

He agrees, and the play ends with a dual renunciation of the man and woman who recognize their duty toward their country and society and stand ready to discharge it at all costs.

Die natürliche Tochter, like *Iphigenie*, has no mob scenes; it is a "Seelendrama," but it is nevertheless essentially social and political. Indeed, the play is so general in application that the characters are called merely the King, the Duke, the Secretary. Even the name of the heroine is general rather than individual, for Eu-genie means highborn.

In a draft for the continuation of the play, Goethe once more puts forward the idea that it is base to follow one's own will; he who is truly noble strives for law and order:[36]

> Nach seinem Sinne leben, ist gemein,
> Der Edle strebt nach Ordnung und Gesetz.

For the most vigorous insistence upon the conversion of the individualist to self-restraint and submission to society

we must, however, return once more to *Faust*. We have seen
that the first part of this drama on the whole depicts the
Sturm-und-Drang individualist who rebels against the limitations of his knowledge and the confines of his human
nature. Faust was striving after the Infinite. It was not one
particular aim for which Faust was striving; for then, perhaps, he might have been satisfied. "Striving" was to him
inescapable; it was part of his nature, just as it is natural to
other men to remain passive and lethargic. As long as Faust
remained Faust, therefore, it was impossible for him to find
peace. The whole world gained significance only as the object
of Faust's titanic activity.

In the second part of *Faust*, however, the world becomes
an independent and active factor. Now for the first time the
hero becomes responsive to influence from the outside world;
thus *Faust* is turned into a "drama of education and development." It is the world, especially the world of Greek mythol-
ogy, which is the educating force that shapes and matures
Faust.

If Gretchen is almost passively hurled down into ruin and
despair, uprooted like a sapling by a storm, Helena holds her
own with Faust, for she is no mere victim of his "titanism."
In the first part Faust plays a predominant part because the
world exists only as the subject of his action; in the second
part Faust dwindles in importance because now the world
has acquired a greater significance. Under the influence of
Helena, and of the Greek world which she represents, Faust
turns to considered, practical activity. In the "Helena" act
itself when the occasion for such action arises, it finds Faust
prepared:

> Nur der verdient die Gunst der Frauen,
> Der kräftigst sie zu schützen weiss.

More striking still is the scene which follows.[37] For here
Faust is tempted by Mephistopheles, as Jesus was tempted

of the devil. All the glories of the world are shown to Faust; but neither the power over countless men, nor the pleasures of a life devoted to love can satisfy him now. Nor does he hanker after infinity, or after the moon. For the first time, he turns instead toward definitely limited spheres:

> Dieser Erdenraum
> Gewährt noch Raum zu grossen Taten.
> Erstaunenswürdiges soll geraten,
> Ich fühle Kraft zu kühnem Fleiss . . .
> Geniessen macht gemein . . .

He becomes determined to wrest a strip of land from the ocean, and his participation in the battles of the emperor (Act IV) serves only to further his new self-restraint and to provide him with the opportunity of completing his scheme.

Not even now, however, has Faust gone the whole way of his development. At the beginning of the fifth act he appears as dissatisfied and restless as ever: Philemon and Baucis must fall victims to his insatiable desire. At this point he begins his final, complete conversion. Thereafter he renounces his ambitions; the superman resigns himself to his human limitations and casts magic aside. Faust, the insatiable individualist, who once sought to live the life of all mankind, now subordinates himself entirely to society. Dying, he envisions the draining of a marsh, and a people who must fight and sacrifice in order to maintain their existence, but who remain free men on free soil:

> Eröffn' ich Räume vielen Millionen,
> Nicht sicher zwar, doch tätig-frei zu wohnen . . .
> Das ist der Weisheit letzter Schluss:
> Nur der verdient sich Freiheit wie das Leben,
> Der täglich sie erobern muss.
> Und so verbringt umrungen von Gefahr,
> Hier Kindheit, Mann und Greis sein tüchtig Jahr.
> Solch ein Gewimmel möcht ich sehn,
> Auf freiem Grund mit freiem Volke stehn.

Faust, like Wilhelm Meister, ends by devoting himself to useful, practical work for others, in which he will survive even after death.

It is clear that neither Mephistopheles nor any other force could satisfy Faust's incessant yearning for the Infinite. And it is equally obvious that self-restraint and devotion to the needs of others would not have satisfied Faust in the beginning. In fact, Faust fails to find any means of assuaging his desires; but, and this is the important point, he resigns himself to this failure. Thus renunciation makes it possible for him to find peace despite his unappeased hunger. This may well be the secret of Faust's end. Until Faust reached the point of resignation, he was necessarily restless and prone to "Sorge." It is Faust, the "Faustian," who says: "Die Sorge nistet gleich im tiefsten Herzen . . ." And it is Faust, forever without peace, the "Stürmer-und-Dränger" whose soul is torn and tormented, whom "Sorge" describes as her victim:

> Soll er gehen, soll er kommen?
> Der Entschluss ist ihm genommen . . .

When "Sorge" asks whether he has ever known her, Faust replies with a description of his restless days, his vain quest:

> Ich bin nur durch die Welt gerannt;
> Ein jed Gelüst ergriff ich bei den Haaren,
> Was nicht genügte, liess ich fahren,
> Was mir entwischte, liess ich ziehn.
> Ich habe nur begehrt und nur vollbracht
> Und abermals gewünscht und so mit Macht
> Mein Leben durchgestürmt; erst gross und mächtig,
> Nun aber geht es weise, geht bedächtig.

With renunciation Faust wins not only peace but victory over "Sorge." Care no longer can beset him.

> Doch deine Macht, o Sorge, schleichend gross,
> Ich werde sie nicht anerkennen.

Thus Faust views his life in retrospect, formulates his new conviction of the necessity of worldly activity and self-restraint, and resigns himself to the pain of unfulfilled desire:

> Nach drüben ist die Aussicht uns verrannt;
> Tor, wer dorthin die Augen blinzelnd richtet,
> Sich über Wolken seinesgleichen dichtet!
> Er stehe fest und sehe hier sich um;
> Dem Tüchtigen ist diese Welt nicht stumm.
> Was braucht er in die Ewigkeit zu schweifen!
> Was er erkennt, lässt sich ergreifen.
> Er wandle so den Erdentag entlang;
> Wenn Geister spuken, geh' er seinen Gang,
> Im Weiterschreiten find er Qual und Glück,
> Er, unbefriedigt jeden Augenblick!

This is the final stage in Faust's metamorphosis: he who had suffered from his own limitations, now postulates that very suffering. Looking back on his own past with a new insight into the necessity of disappointment and resignation, Faust sees his own tragedy with the eyes of an unconcerned spectator. And with this new understanding of his own character and his sufferings, he can in a sense stand aside to observe the conflict within him. He has achieved aloofness, can see his own internal struggle as the Lord looked upon it in the "Vorspiel," and as Goethe, in his classical and mature period, saw it when writing the "Vorspiel." Having acknowledged the necessity of self-restraint, Faust ceases to suffer from it; and in his very recognition of the necessity of suffering, he ceases to suffer from that necessity.

Faust succeeds where Tasso failed. He learns renunciation: he can manage to look at himself objectively and thereby to overcome subjectivism and individualism. In this respect, as in so many others, Faust reflects Goethe's own development. Like Faust, Goethe reviewed his life objectively. He wrote his autobiography and postulated in it once more the necessity of renunciation. The following passage from *Dichtung und Wahrheit* may well serve to summarize and conclude our investigation into Goethe's ideal of renunciation and social adaptation:[38]

Unser physisches sowohl als geselliges Leben, Sitten, Gewohnheiten, Weltklugheit, Philosophie, Religion, ja so manches zufällige Ereignis, alles ruft uns zu, dass wir entsagen sollen. So manches was uns innerlich eigenst angehört, sollen wir nicht nach aussen hervorbilden; was vir von aussen zur Ergänzung unsres Wesens bedürfen, wird uns entzogen, dagegen aber so vieles aufgedrungen, das uns so fremd als lästig ist. Man beraubt uns des mühsam Erworbenen, des freundlich Gestatteten, und ehe wir hierüber recht ins Klare sind, finden wir uns genötigt, unsere Persönlichkeit erst stückweise und dann völlig aufzugeben.

And one must preserve classical poise and serenity:

Dabei ist es aber hergebracht, dass man denjenigen nicht achtet, der sich deshalb ungebärdig stellt; vielmehr soll man, je bittrer der Kelch ist, eine desto süssere Miene machen, damit ja der gelassene Zuschauer nicht durch irgendeine Grimasse beleidigt werde.

SCHILLER

The note of heroism so characteristic of classical self-denial is sounded almost too noisily by Schiller. In nearly all his dramas there is to be found a character who becomes a "hero" by realizing that he must fulfill his duty and obey the law, with which indeed he eventually identifies himself.

The most apt illustration of this tenet, however, is to be found not in a play but in the ballad "Der Kampf mit dem Drachen" (1798). A dragon devastates the country, but because many brave men have already lost their lives in seeking to slay it, the Master of the Order of St. John forbids any further attempt. Nevertheless, a knight of the Order, with great courage and perspicacity, does succeed in killing the dragon. Despite the fact that he is hailed as a savior by the populace, he is severely reprimanded by the Master and expelled from the Order. He has killed the dragon, to be sure, but he has also fostered an evil far worse, one which poisons the heart and leads to discord and destruction. He has, in short, encouraged obstinacy and rebelliousness. For it is not courage but obedience which is the prime virtue of a Christian:

> Den Drachen, der dies Land
> Verheert, schlugst Du mit tapfrer Hand;
> Ein Gott bist Du dem Volke worden,
> Ein Feind kommst du zurück dem Orden,
> Und einen schlimmern Wurm gebar
> Dein Herz, als dieser Drache war.
> Die Schlange, die das Herz vergiftet,
> Die Zwietracht und Verderben stiftet,
> Das ist der widerspenst'ge Geist,
> Der gegen Zucht sich frech empöret,
> Der Ordnung heilig Band zerreisst;
> Denn der ist's, der die Welt zerstöret.

> Mut zeigt auch der Mameluck,
> Gehorsam ist des Christen Schmuck.

Only when the knight acknowledges the absolute supremacy of law and authority, when he divests himself voluntarily of the insignia of his Order does he regain the right to membership in the Order:

> Dir ist der härt're Kampf gelungen.
> Nimm dieses Kreuz! Es ist der Lohn
> Der Demut, die sich selbst bezwungen.

Don Carlos, the play which signalizes Schiller's rejection of Sturm-und-Drang and his conversion to classicism, clearly expresses the new conception of duty and renunciation. Marquis Posa sacrifices himself for Carlos and for his country; the Queen, too, foregoes personal happiness and love for the sake of the nation. And Carlos, exhorted by both the Queen and Posa, renounces his love, and bows to his duty toward the state. Here we have a typical triumvirate of Schillerian heroes. Duty triumphant—such is the classical attitude. And Posa's famous tirade in defense of Freedom is no claim of free action for the individual in the manner of the Sturm-und-Drang, but an insistence upon human dignity and equal rights for all men. Marquis Posa is not an individualist, but an idealist who advocates the Rights of Man. Nor does he play the role of the great individual hampered by society and eventually destroyed by it. His death is the glorification of an order higher than the individual, and not a challenge to it.

It is instructive to observe the changes which the concept of "freedom" underwent during the transition from Sturm-und-Drang to classicism, or from Schiller's early plays to his later ones. In *Die Räuber, Fiesco, Kabale und Liebe*, and even in *Don Carlos*, freedom is political or physical in essence, and can be wrested from the tyrants and oppressors of this world. But in Schiller's later plays freedom is a metaphysical quality, and can neither be withheld nor granted by any force outside man himself. "Freedom" does not imply liberation "from" anything: it means merely that man is free "to" do his duty and to comply with the moral law.

This higher freedom is the basic theme of Schiller's *Wallenstein*. Here the protagonist could well have served as the hero of a typical Sturm-und-Drang play: the unique man who arrogates to himself the right to break the law and to flout the rights of others for the sake of his mission, and whose ultimate failure would constitute a bitter indictment of a world so petty that it stifles the man of genius. Representing Schiller's true mind, however, is Max, who limits his activities strictly to the performance of his duty. And furthermore Wallenstein himself is fully aware of the significance of law and order; indeed it is this very acknowledgment which paralyzes his activity and causes him to procrastinate. Wallenstein never actually violates the law but merely contemplates doing so; yet since he has sinned in thought, his death in propitiation of the law is justified.

Schiller's next play, *Maria Stuart*, devotes four acts to Maria's fight for life and the fifth to her resignation. Maria has committed a single sin, long since confessed and repented, but she is innocent of the crime of which she is accused and for which she is to die at the hands of her enemies. In the last act, Maria, reconciled with heaven and earth, forgives her enemies, renounces both her love and her right to the throne, and accepts an undeserved death as punishment for her early crime:

> Gott würdigt mich durch diesen unverdienten Tod
> Die frühe schwere Blutschuld abzubüssen.
>
> (V, 7)

She dies not as a victim of law and order but for the greater glory of these institutions, and by her sacrifice achieves the highest degree of "heroism."

The value of self-abnegation and subservience to higher commands is shown still more clearly in *Die Jungfrau von Orleans*. Joan of Arc has been entrusted with a divine mission. She has been chosen to free her country and to crown its king. She must pursue this single purpose and avoid any indulgence of personal emotions. From the very beginning it is clear that she is merely obeying the call to duty:

> So ist des Geistes Ruf an mich ergangen,
> Mich treibt nicht eitles, irdisches Verlangen.
>
> (Prolog, 4)

> . . . Ich *muss*—mich treibt die Götterstimme, nicht
> Eignes Gelüsten—*euch* zu bitterm Harm, *mir* nicht
> Zur Freude . . .
>
> (II, 7)

Queen Isabeau, in sharp contrast to Joan, knows no law but her own impulse:

Ich habe Leidenschaften, warmes Blut
Wie eine andre, und ich kam als Königin
In dieses Land, zu leben, nicht zu scheinen.
Sollt' ich der Freud' absterben, weil der Fluch
Des Schicksals meine lebensfrohe Jugend
Zu dem wahnsinn'gen Gatten hat gesellt?
Mehr als das Leben lieb' ich meine Freiheit . . .

(II, 2)

Schiller is not satisfied to allow Joan to remain a blind tool, to kill Montgomery and complete her task. She must reach a climax of final renunciation. Here the moral is pointed with almost mathematical precision: Joan deviates from the designated path, allows personal emotion to sway her, and thus becomes culpable. Because of her guilt, however, she voluntarily sacrifices her love and abandons every purely personal desire, for only thus can she attain to truly "heroic" stature. Having won a decisive victory over herself in this internal struggle, Joan can now calmly face even the man who had caused her to falter. Submitting to a superior force, she expiates her transgression by her death.

Die Braut von Messina, Schiller's next play, might appear at first glance a fatalistic tragedy in the manner of the Greeks. But here Don Cesar, who has murdered his brother, accepts full responsibility for his crime. By his death he atones for the murder and at the same time shakes off the shackles of fate. This denouement may not be in harmony with the Greek conception of fate, but it illustrates once more the typically Schillerian doctrine of duty. By self-denial and submission to the eternal, super-individual law, the individual becomes a "hero."

In his last complete play Schiller expressly contrasts the struggle for individual liberty with obedience to moral law. It is not personal interest or desire which impels Wilhelm Tell to free his country from the tyrant; it is recognition of a duty which he must fulfill even against his own inclination. As Tell sees it: "Der brave Mann denkt an sich selbst zuletzt." He is neither impulsive nor rash, and if he commits murder his deed is nevertheless just and unselfish. Tell, like any other Schillerian hero, does no more than his duty. This fact would have been clear even without the fifth act, in which Tell, announcing that *his* hand is clean, refuses to touch that of Johannes Parricida—a scene which borders on Pharisaism. It need not concern us here whether Schiller was altogether successful in establishing the difference between the just political murder and the unjust. It must be assumed that Tell's cause is just, for the moral of the play is that Tell, by accepting the unpleasant duty of committing murder, has thereby succeeded in restoring the order which the tyrant disturbed.

In his rigid doctrines of duty, his insistence upon the supreme moral law, Schiller clearly reveals the influence of Kant. Kant's categorical imperative is perhaps the most striking formulation of the subordination of the individual to the general law. It implies that the individual must adjust himself to society. According to Kant, everyone should act in such a way that the principle of his action may serve as the principle of a general law. The individual is reduced to a unit in the fabric of society—a direct contradiction of the Sturm-und-Drang precept that the exceptional man has exceptional rights.

When Schiller first tackled Kant's philosophy, he sought to reconcile the German's stern, rigid morality with Shaftesbury's philosophy of beauty and love. Similarly the romanticists later attempted to water down the Kantian philosophy. But although in both cases there was almost the same degree of dilution of Kantianism with foreign philosophy, each had a different historical significance: Schiller was moving toward Kant, the romanticists were drawing away from him.

Schiller never glorified civic society so unequivocally as

did Goethe, yet it is the former who has become the poet of the middle classes. It was Schiller who set the burgher on a pedestal, there to remain until Nietzsche knocked him off. In Schiller's plays the burgher found glorified all the virtues which he recognized as his own distinctive qualities. Schiller's sententiousness, his rhetoric and his verbosity were admired and imitated.

There remains one of Schiller's poems in praise of "Bürgertum" which can still hold its own, even with Goethe's *Hermann und Dorothea*. This is his "Lied von der Glocke," in which he eulogizes a manual worker, the bell-founder. Observing that the bell tolls on the birth and death and marriage of men, Schiller introduces detailed descriptions of the pleasures and tribulations of domestic life, the joys and sorrows recurrent in the family circle, and the peace and contentment characteristic of the middle-class home:

> Arbeit ist des Bürgers Zierde,
> Segen ist der Mühe Preis;
> Ehrt den König seine Würde,
> Ehret uns der Hände Fleiss.

No popular anthology is complete without this poem. Middle-class girls and boys still learn it by heart and are moved by its pathos. But when it was recited for the first time in a romantic salon, the guests all but collapsed with laughter.[39]

ROMANTICISM: COMMUNITY

THE ISOLATION OF THE INDIVIDUAL AND THE EARLY ROMANTIC CONCEPTION OF LOVE

THE classicist, as we have observed, envisages a social order to which the individual must adapt himself by renunciation and self-restraint. The romanticist, on the other hand, looks to an association of free individuals joined together in perfect union. Modifying the sociological classification introduced by Ferdinand Tönnies,[40] we may perhaps use the term "community" to denote this romantic ideal, in contrast to the classical "society."

Community does not involve submergence or restraint on the part of the individual, but merely membership in and full development within the community. To the community the individual contributes that which he and he alone can give; for the community depends on individually differentiated men just as the organism depends on its discrete and specialized organs.

The romantic desire for common and joint action, for the "SYN"—sym-pathize, sym-philosophize, sym-poetize[41]— was based upon a concept of collective and mutual assistance, not upon classical subordination to the law. This ideal of "coaction" corresponds perhaps most closely to the coöperation of members of an academy or scholars of a university who, by pursuing their own intellectual interests, yet serve to aid one another. The community is a "Republic of free men." It does not demand of its members self-denial and self-renunciation as does the state or society, but on the contrary allows them free development and self-fulfillment.

There is an essential difference between classical society and romantic community. The romanticists cannot glorify civic society, but neither do they return to the individualism of the Sturm-und-Drang; they look forward to another golden age, a revival of happy human community in which love and good will, not duty and principles, are the controlling forces. It is this orientation which explains the religious tinge in so many romantic writings.

If Kant, in his categorical imperative, formulated the ethical and social creed of classicism, Schleiermacher, in his *Monologen,* expresses that of romanticism. According to Schleiermacher, it is the duty of man, and especially of the artist, to express himself, not at the cost of the community but in coöperation with it:

Bewege alles in der Welt, und richte aus, was du vermagst; gib dich hin dem Gefühl deiner angebornen Schranken, bearbeite jedes Mittel der geistigen Gemeinschaft; stelle dar dein Eigentümliches, und zeichne mit deinem Geist alles was dich umgibt; arbeite an den heiligen Werken der Menschheit, ziehe an die befreundeten Geister: aber immer schaue in dich selbst, wisse was du tust, und in welcher Gestalt dein Handeln einhergeht.

And Schleiermacher actually contrasts the ideal community of men free to follow the spirit which informs them with a society based on mutual self-sacrifice:

Es seufzet, was zur bessern Welt gehört in düsterer Sklaverei! Was da ist von geistiger Gemeinschaft, ist herabgewürdigt zum Dienst der irdischen; nur dieser nützlich wirkt es dem Geiste Beschränkung, tut dem innern Leben Abbruch. Wenn der Freund dem Freunde die Hand zum Bündnis reicht: es sollten Taten draus hervorgehen, grösser als jeder Einzelne; frei sollte jeder jeden gewähren lassen, wozu der Geist ihn treibt, und nur sich hülfreich zeigen wo es jenem fehlt, nicht seinem Gedanken den eignen unterschiebend. So fände jeder im andern Leben und Nahrung, und was er werden könnte, würd' er ganz. Wie treiben sie es dagegen in der Welt? Zum irdischen Dienst ist einer stets dem andern gewärtig,

bereit das eigne Wohlsein aufzuopfern; und Erkenntnis mitzu-
teilen, Gefühle mitzuleiden und zu lindern, ist das Höchste.

The early romanticists sought a world in which the individual's rights would be restored to him. Whereas Goethe,
in his *Wahlverwandtschaften*, had announced the superiority
of law over passion, Friedrich Schlegel, in his *Lucinde*, now
pleads for the legitimacy of love. Love—and this is the main
point of the novel—is both sensuous and spiritual. Love is a
strong, almost religious force in that it lends depth and significance to life and transports man to a plane of bodily and
spiritual rapture comparable to that of extreme religious ex-
altation. Love literally creates paradise on earth in the harmonious and ecstatic union of two lovers. *Lucinde* has often
been regarded as the expression of crude individualism and
voluptuous egotism. But though it may be deficient both in
taste and in artistic perfection, the state of perfect harmony
which it describes is set forth with a faith so sincere that it
cannot fail to be translated, at least in some degree, to the
reader.[42] Schlegel's conception of love, the primeval form of
"social relation," reflects very clearly the new social ideals.
In Sturm-und-Drang individualism is militant, overbearing,
ruthless: the individual is bent on the gratification of his
senses and instincts. In classicism love is subject to the
general law, and the individual is subordinate to the social
order. In romanticism love is the ideal communion of two or
more persons, the very essence of community. For the romanticist marriage without love is sin, while the union of two
lovers may become almost a kind of religious worship. It is
this ultimate metaphysical significance which distinguishes
the romantic conception of love from the Sturm-und-Drang
"Sich-Ausleben."

Similar in theme and subject to Schlegel's *Lucinde* is Brentano's novel, *Godwi*, perhaps the most outstanding example
of both romantic irony and formlessness. Godwi, like Wil-

helm Meister, sets out to travel and at each stage of his journey finds another woman with whom he falls in love: Lady Molly Hodefield, Ioduno von Eichenwehen, Ottilie Senne. Wilhelm, however, even before he began his travels, had a deeper sense of responsibility than Godwi will ever have. Godwi remains substantially unchanged throughout the novel; he is as subjective and individualistic in the end as he was in the beginning. In a letter to his friend Römer, he violently attacks bourgeois civic society, also like Wilhelm Meister, and insists upon the right to follow his own inclinations: "Leben ist eine Freikunst, ich treibe sie wo und wie ich will." But Godwi never finds the way into human society as Wilhelm Meister does; on the contrary the recipient of his letter ceases to be a philistine burgher and becomes an individualist like Godwi. And Lady Hodefield not only devotes her own life to individualistic self-fulfillment but advocates it for others, especially for the artist: "Menschen mit voller Lebensfähigkeit, und so auch ich, stehen immer im Kampfe mit dem geregelten Leben. Sie sind bloss für das Dasein und nicht für den Staat gebildet." Here also the poet Maria, in contemplating a monument to a courtesan, is inspired to express his most lascivious reveries and to voice strong objections to civil marriage. Indeed the very fact that a monument to a courtesan had been erected is significant. Interesting, too, is Godwi's enunciation of the precept: "be yourself":

Es klingt paradox, sagte ich, aber es ist doch wahr, wer zur Wollust geboren ist und sie nicht übt, führt ein recht lasterhaftes Leben. Es ist nichts Unkeuscheres als ein recht sinnliches Mädchen, das keusch ist, und eine Violette, die sich bekehrt, verliert ihre Unschuld. Der Staat aber ist nur auf eine Gattung eingerichtet, und besteht aus sehr schlechten Menschen, weil ein Teil gut, und der andere schlecht werden *muss*, um tugendhaft zu sein, wie es der Staat will.

All this sounds like Heinse's extreme individualism, and it is certainly a marked reaction against the classical teaching of "renunciation." But the argument put forward by Kluckhohn for a more charitable interpretation of Schlegel's *Lucinde* would also apply to *Godwi;* in general the lasciviousness and extreme subjectivism of this novel probably reflect literary tradition rather than genuine conviction on the part of the author. And Brentano himself qualifies his remarks to some extent through his irony. In the second part of the book the poet meets the characters of his novel; they comment upon themselves, correcting and amplifying the poet's statements. Now it appears that two persons are one and the same: the characters are interchangeable. By virtue of this tone of ironic aloofness the poet declines responsibility for the morals of the novel. And then there are other characters who evidently enjoy more of the poet's approbation than Godwi and Lady Hodefield, namely, Cornelia-Annonciata and Joseph-Werdo, two saintlike personages. Thus Lady Hodefield is saved from excess and dissipation by Werdo. She acknowledges his beneficial influence, but at the same time demands the right to live her own life:

Sie haben mich gelehrt, meine Handlungen nach allgemeinen Gesetzen um der Ruhe und Ordnung willen zu beschränken, ohne deswegen meine Art zu fühlen, welche die Eigentümlichkeit meines Zusammenhangs mit der Natur bestimmt, zu erdrücken—und auch ohnedies ist es mir nie möglich gewesen, mich wie eine Bürgerin in die freie Welt hineinzuheucheln, das Gepräge meiner Seele ist zu tief, es konnte nicht erlöschen, und ich bin schon in so weit vor der Verfolgung der Bürgertugend geschützt, als man von mir, einer reichen Engländerin, sonderbare Streiche prätendiert.

Brentano's ideal is not self-assertion for its own sake, but free, unhampered existence within the perfect community. And if his characters cannot live within a community since this community does not yet exist, this isolation of the individual is felt to be a tragic curse. Godwi's father yearns, even in the embrace of love, for the universe. Godwi himself strives to establish some relationship to the whole of mankind; Lady Hodefield wants his way to be a way of expansion. Not of their own choice, but because their yearning is forever unsatisfied, are these men lonely and unhappy. Eusebio represents the embodiment of this unstilled longing:

Er öffnet die Arme mit Sehnsucht und nimmer kann er mehr umarmen als sich selbst, so entsteht bei immer neuen Versuchen und einem steten Zurückkehren ohne Erfolg diese entsagende Trauer in ihm.

AIMLESSNESS AND POETIC LIFE

Just as the romanticists reject the subordination of the individual in love, so also they do oppose his devotion to one limited sphere of activity. The romantic aimlessness and passivity contrast sharply with the almost utilitarian purposefulness of the leading characters in *Wilhelm Meister*. Thus in *Lucinde* we find the familiar passage in praise of idleness:

O Müssiggang, Müssiggang! du bist die Lebenslust der Unschuld und der Begeisterung; dich atmen die Seligen, und selig ist, wer dich hat und hegt, du heiliges Kleinod! einziges Fragment von Gottähnlichkeit, das uns noch aus dem Paradies blieb.

To consummate expression of this romantic aimlessness is, of course, Eichendorff's *Aus dem Leben eines Taugenichts*. Neither Schlegel's rhapsody nor Eichendorff's tale is to be taken too seriously, however, since both contain a goodly measure of irony. Even so, the contrast with Goethe's religion of activity remains striking enough.

The romantic novel and "Novelle" deal not so much with the conflict between the individual and the world as with the development of the individual within the world. The world of the romanticists is not the hostile force it was in *Werther*, but rather the necessary medium for the hero's growth, as in

Wilhelm Meister. Here at least romanticism seems to build on classical tradition rather than on that of the Sturm-und-Drang. Characters like Tieck's Sternbald, Dorothea Schlegel's Florentin, Novalis' Heinrich von Ofterdingen, or Eichendorff's Friedrich (in *Ahnung und Gegenwart*) travel about a world which is essentially unrealistic and poetic. The romantic hero does not shun the world; yet critics have called romantic literature a "literature of escape," because it ignores the utilitarian world of classicism, the world of toil and duty, in which Goethe's Wilhelm Meister and Faust, for example, sought to anchor their existence. The romantic hero has no profession and no need to earn a living; he dwells in a sphere where leisure and liberty prevail.

Such romantic unreality pervades Eichendorff's *Ahnung und Gegenwart,* although this novel in many respects foreshadows the realist school. The title itself expresses a reorientation toward the present, toward the here-and-now. And the hero, in a conversation with the poet Faber (Chapter III), protests against a poetry of make-believe, chiding the poets for bewailing the past and disregarding the present. Again, in discussing Arnim's *Dolores,* he insists that poetry must not lose touch with life (Chapter XII). Friedrich even tries to win the prince for his plans and thus bring them nearer materialization (Chapter XIV). Nevertheless, the book itself depicts a world unreal and fundamentally romantic. Friedrich travels about at will, following Rosa, stopping at Leontin's castle, setting out again with Leontin or alone; always engaged in a series of casual encounters, he meets one character, then another, finding himself unexpectedly in a new place from which he departs once more. Finally Leontin goes to America and Rudolf to Egypt, the country of magic, while Friedrich himself enters a monastery.

Despite Eichendorff's emphasis on "Gegenwart," Friedrich's travels are not unlike those of the *Taugenichts.*

NOVALIS

Goethe's *Wilhelm Meister* exerted a marked influence upon
German romantic literature; but it was the style, the treatment, the technique, rather than the thoughts expressed
therein, which appealed to the romanticists. The insistence
upon self-limitation and conformity to the requirements of
society must have seemed to them somewhat Philistine.

Novalis, once an enthusiastic admirer of the novel, began,
indeed, to attack it. His *Ofterdingen* was conceived and written expressly as a contrast to *Wilhelm Meister,* which he
assailed also in a letter to Tieck, dated February 23, 1800.

In particular he was repelled by Goethe's transition from
poetry to economics:

So viel ich auch aus "Meister" gelernt habe und noch lerne, so
odiös ist doch im Grunde das ganze Buch . . . Es ist ein "Can-
dide" gegen die Poesie—ein nobilitierter Roman . . . Das Buch ist
unendlich merkwürdig—aber man freut sich doch herzlich, wenn
man von der ängstlichen Peinlichkeit des vierten Teils erlöst und
zum Schluss gekommen ist . . . Ich wollte noch viel darüber sagen,
denn es ist mir alles so klar und ich sehe so deutlich die grosse
Kunst, mit der die Poesie durch sich selbst im "Meister" vernichtet
wird—und während sie im Hintergrund scheitert, die Ökonomie
sicher auf festem Grund und Boden mit ihren Freunden sich güt-
lich tut und achselzuckend nach dem Meere sieht.

And in Novalis' notebook there is a similar entry:[43]

Es ist im Grunde ein fatales und albernes Buch—so pretentiös und
pretiös—undichterisch im höchsten Grade, was den Geist betrifft—
so poetisch auch die Darstellung ist. Es ist eine Satire auf die
Poesie, Religion etc. Aus Stroh und Hobelspänen ein wohlschmek-
kendes Gericht, ein Götterbild zusammengesetzt. Hinten wird alles
Farce. Die ökonomische Natur ist die wahre—übrigbleibende . . .

Der Abbé ist ein fataler Kerl, dessen geheime Oberaufsicht lästig
und lächerlich wird. Der Turm in Lotharios Schlosse ist ein grosser
Widerspruch mit demselben . . .

Der Held retardiert das Eindringen des Evangeliums der Ökonomie. Marionettentheater im Anfang. Der Schluss ist wie die letzten Stunden im Park der schönen Lili.

If Novalis takes such violent exception to the "Ökonomie" in *Die Lehrjahre*, it is not difficult to imagine what he might have said about *Die Wanderjahre*, the first part of which appeared some twenty years after his letter to Tieck.

Novalis never completed his *Ofterdingen;* but the first part and the fragment of the second indicate clearly that he looked forward to a society diametrically opposed to that which represented Goethe's ideal. *Heinrich von Ofterdingen*, like *Wilhelm Meister*, is a novel of development and education. Journeying from Eisenach to Augsburg to pay a visit to his grandfather, the hero meets a series of individuals who personify different aspects of life, so that every new encounter is like the opening of another door within him. In Augsburg he becomes acquainted with Klingsohr, who initiates him into the secrets of poetry. Here too he meets Mathilda, and in his love for her he reaches the culmination of his education. Her death, of which he learns in a dream, leaves him a mature poet.

The second, unfinished, part of the novel was to depict Heinrich's career as poet and the dawn of a new world, the world of poetry. In contrast to Goethe's "Entsagung," Novalis sought to present "Die Erfüllung." Heinrich was to inaugurate a new golden age, to destroy the power of the sun and the seasons, to unite all opposites—night and day, north and south, youth and age, past and future. The second part, then, opens with the song of Astralis, who had been conceived in the first embrace of Heinrich and Mathilde. Here the ideal community, the new golden age is depicted:

> Es bricht die neue Welt herein
> Und verdunkelt den hellsten Sonnenschein,
> Man sieht nun aus bemoosten Trümmern

Eine wunderseltsame Zukunft schimmern,
Und was vordem alltäglich war,
Scheint jetzo fremd und wunderbar.
(Eins in allem und alles in Einen
Gottes Bild auf Kräutern und Steinen
Gottes Geist in Menschen und Tieren,
Dies muss man sich zu Gemüte führen.
Keine Ordnung mehr nach Raum und Zeit
Hier Zukunft in der Vergangenheit.)
Der Liebe Reich ist aufgetan,
Die Fabel fängt zu spinnen an.
Das Urspiel jeder Natur beginnt,
Auf kräftige Worte jedes sinnt,
Und so das grosse Weltgemüt
Überall sich regt und unendlich blüht.
Alles muss in einander greifen,
Eins durch das andre gedeihn und reifen;
Jedes in allen dar sich stellt,
Indem es sich mit ihnen vermischet
Und gierig in ihre Tiefen fällt,
Sein eigentümliches Wesen erfrischet
Und tausend neue Gedanken erhält.
Die Welt wird Traum, der Traum wird Welt,
Und was man glaubt, es sei geschehn,
Kann man von weitem erst kommen sehn.
Frei soll die Phantasie erst schalten,
Nach ihren Gefallen die Fäden verweben,
Hier manches verschleiern, dort manches entfalten,
Und endlich in magischen Dunst verschweben.
Wehmut und Wollust, Tod und Leben
Sind hier in innigster Sympathie—
Wer sich der höchsten Lieb' ergeben,
Genest von ihren Wunden nie.
Schmerzhaft muss jenes Band zerreissen,
Was sich ums innre Auge zieht,
Einmal das treuste Herz verwaisen,
Eh es der trüben Welt entflieht.
Der Leib wird aufgelöst in Tränen,
Zum weiten Grabe wird die Welt,

In das, verzehrt von bangem Sehnen,
Das Herz, als Asche, niederfällt.

The utopia described here was foreshadowed in the first part of the novel in a story told by Klingsohr. The characters in Klingsohr's tale were to have reappeared in the second part, concluding with the reign of Eros and the eternal golden age.[44]

At the beginning of the second part Henrich, encountering the aged Sylvester, asks: "When will there be no more fear, pain, need, and evil?" And Sylvester replies: "When there is only one power—the power of conscience." Conscience, that is, the freedom of the master who determines his actions and is not restricted by them. Conscience, that is, man's particular nature and not something general:

Und gerade diese allumfassende Freiheit, Meisterschaft oder Herrschaft ist das Wesen, der Trieb des Gewissens. In ihm offenbart sich die heilige Eigentümlichkeit, das unmittelbare Schaffen der Persönlichkeit, und jede Handlung des Meisters ist zugleich Kundwerdung der hohen, einfachen, unverwickelten Welt—Gottes Wort. . . . Das Gewissen ist der Menschen eigenstes Wesen in voller Verklärung, der himmlische Urmensch. Es ist nicht dies und jenes, es gebietet nicht in allgemeinen Sprüchen, es besteht nicht aus einzelnen Tugenden. Es gibt nur *eine* Tugend—den reinen, ernsten Willen, der im Augenblick der Entscheidung unmittelbar sich entschliesst und wählt. In lebendiger, eigentümlicher Unteilbarkeit bewohnt es und beseelt es das zärtliche Sinnbild des menschlichen Körpers und vermag alle geistigen Gliedmassen in die wahrhafteste Tätigkeit zu versetzen.

As in *Ofterdingen* the anticipation of a millennium, of a New Jerusalem where love should reign supreme and where all mankind and all nature should be harmoniously united, also permeates the *Hymnen an die Nacht,* especially the fifth hymn.

It is apparent that the community envisaged by Novalis has nothing in common with Goethe's concept of society. The individual in Novalis' poems is not called upon to learn renunciation. In fact, Novalis is not concerned primarily with the development of Heinrich or of any other individual, but rather with the development of humanity from a "dark age" to a "golden age," from imperfect society to community.

HÖLDERLIN

Hölderlin, like Novalis, dreams of a golden age, but his vision is less mystical, less obscure; and his social ideal is more clearly defined. For Hölderlin the highest form of human relationship is the community, where every individual dwells in harmonious union with every other. The individual here is by no means obliged to give up his own individuality; on the contrary, it is only within the community that he can grow to full stature.[45]

> immer besteht ein Mass,
> Allen gemein, doch jeglichem auch ist eignes beschieden,
> Dahin gehet und kommt jeder, wohin er es kann.
>
> ("Brot und Wein")

The oak grove symbolizes Hölderlin's ideal of community; each oak tree grows untended by man, wild and strong and free, like one of the Titans. Each is a world of its own; yet they all grow and live together in a free union like the stars in the sky, everyone a god:

> Keiner von euch ist noch in die Schule der Menschen gegangen,
> Und ihr drängt euch fröhlich und frei, aus der kräftigen Wurzel,
> Untereinander herauf und ergreift, wie der Adler die Beute,
> Mit gewaltigem Arme den Raum, und gegen die Wolken
> Ist euch heiter und gross die sonnige Krone gerichtet.
> Eine Welt ist jeder von euch, wie die Sterne des Himmels
> Lebt ihr, jeder ein Gott, in freiem Bunde zusammen.
>
> ("Die Eichbäume")

According to Hölderlin the Greeks actually achieved this ideal community. Again and again he sings of the golden age of Greece, where there prevailed a harmonious union of free men, and not, as Goethe saw it, merely artistic perfection.[46]

Hölderlin's nostalgia for Greece springs mainly from this source; he never ceases to reproach his fellow-Germans for being narrowly limited, each to his own sphere, instead of establishing a relationship with mankind as a whole. Thus in a letter dated January 1, 1799, Hölderlin writes to his brother:

Und wie nur der in seiner Stube sich gefällt, der auch im freien Felde lebt, so kann ohne Allgemeinsinn und offnen Blick in die Welt auch das individuelle, jedem eigene Leben nicht bestehen, und wirklich ist unter den Deutschen eines mit dem andern untergegangen, wie es scheint . . .

Here he states expressly that the spirit of community does not impair, but actually conditions, the freedom and self-determination of the individual. He proceeds, furthermore, to attribute to art and poetry the function of bringing men together in a harmony which permits each individual to express his own peculiar character:

Sie (die Kunst) nähert die Menschen und bringt sie zusammen, nicht wie das Spiel, wo sie nur dadurch vereiniget sind, dass jeder sich vergisst und die lebendige Eigentümlichkeit von keinem zum Vorschein kommt . . .

And

. . . so hat die philosophisch-politische Bildung schon in sich selbst die Inkonvenienz, dass sie zwar die Menschen zu den wesentlichen, unumgänglich notwendigen Verhältnissen, zu Pflicht und Recht zusammenknüpft, aber wieviel ist dann zur Menschenharmonie noch übrig?

This "community" as conceived by Hölderlin and the romanticists, in which the "Eigentümlichkeit," or individuality is preserved, is almost diametrically opposed to the classical conception of "Entsagung," of obedience and duty, whereby the individual is called upon to forego his godlike autonomy. Hölderlin always regarded himself as a poet entrusted with the high mission of serving as leader and prophet, guiding his people toward the goal of an ideal human community. He disparages the German and extols the Greek, but his great ambition is to rekindle the light of Greece in Germany. In his elegy, "Der Archipelagus," Hölderlin presents his view of Greece. He sees the defeat and magnificent recovery of Athens at the time of the Persian wars; he complains that Hellas is dead, and he yearns for its ideal community. At the same time he denounces his contemporaries for knowing only their own work, for their enslavement to their narrow interests and occupations. A similarly bitter denunciation of German barbarism is to be found in the famous closing passage of the novel, *Hyperion,* but "Der Archipelagus," like many of Hölderlin's other poems, ends with a prophetic picture of the time when the modern nations will emerge from their egocentricity to the ideal community of freedom, humanity, and love—when Greece will be reborn in Germany:

> Denn es ruhn die Himmlischen gern am fühlenden Herzen,
> Immer, wie sonst, geleiten sie noch, die begeisternden Kräfte,
> Gerne den strebenden Mann, und über den Bergen der Heimat
> Ruht und waltet und lebt allgegenwärtig der Äther,
> Dass ein liebendes Volk, in des Vaters Armen gesammelt,
> Menschlich freudig, wie sonst, und *ein* Geist allen gemein sei.

Hyperion, the hero of Hölderlin's novel, takes up arms against the Turks to reëstablish a community like that of ancient Greece. It is his bitter disappointment in this endeavor which causes him to withdraw from all human society. The problem of an ideal human community, therefore, is the central theme of the novel. But the human community is, for Hölderlin, inseparably connected, and in fact identical, with a new pantheistic nature worship.[47] For only through a new religion can men again be united in a holy community. The conception of a primeval golden age, where men lived in happy harmony with nature and in ideal community with each other, Hölderlin acquired, both directly and indirectly, from Rousseau. This natural state of harmony, though once lost, must eventually be reëstablished by human effort and education,[48] a millennial hope which Hölderlin expresses in his preface to the novel. We have lost the state of childhood and must now strive after perfection:[49]

Jenen ewigen Widerstreit zwischen uns selbst und der Welt zu endigen, den Frieden alles Friedens, der höher ist denn alle Vernunft, den wiederzubringen, uns mit der Natur zu vereinigen, zu Einem unendlichen Ganzen, das ist das Ziel all' unseres Strebens, wir mögen uns darüber verstehen oder nicht.

Hyperion longs for ancient Greece and yearns to be one with nature: "Eines zu sein mit allem, was lebt!" Again and again he recalls the peace, harmony, and innocence of his childhood. After an enthusiastic friendship with Adamas, he meets Alabanda, who like himself resents the degradation of the modern Greek. Very characteristically Hyperion, in a discussion with Alabanda, denounces the state as based on compulsion and opposed to the free community,[50] and because Alabanda supports the state and associates with a group of reformers who believe in force and coercion, the friendship is ruptured. After this painful disillusionment Hyperion finds happiness for a time in his love for Diotima. But again, very characteristically, this union proves too circumscribed; it must be extended to comprise all mankind and even the whole universe. Interesting also is the fact that it is Diotima herself who warns Hyperion not to lock himself up in the heaven of his life but to fulfill his mission.[51] In one of his poems Hölderlin compares love to a plant; just as the plant would grow into a forest, so the harmony between two lovers should evolve into a universal harmony:

Wachs' und werde zum Wald! eine beseeltere,
Vollentblühende Welt! Sprache der Liebenden
Sei die Sprache des Landes,
Ihre Seele der Laut des Volkes!

Together with Diotima, Hyperion visits the ruins of Athens

where once the ideal community flourished, and here, in the very center of the novel, he expounds his views on the ideal human community.[52] The Spartans, he says, were kept under strict discipline; in the Orient despotism rules; in the North reason and intellect govern. But reason and intellect are only slave drivers; they keep order through the stern application of law:

Des Verstandes ganzes Geschäft ist Notwerk. Vor dem Unsinn, vor dem Unrecht schützt er uns, indem er ordnet; aber sicher zu sein vor Unsinn und vor Unrecht ist doch nicht die höchste Stufe menschlicher Vortrefflichkeit.

Nowhere does there prevail the harmony and oneness of humanity characteristic of Athens. In words strongly reminiscent of the classicist,[52] Hölderlin praises the achievement of the happy medium between extremes, the "wholeness" and perfection of the Athenians. It is most significant, however, that whereas for the classicist this harmony took place within the individual ("Der Mensch"), for Hölderlin it becomes manifest within the human community.

Hyperion joins in the fight for Greek independence against the Turk. But he is destined to bitter disappointment and disillusionment: his followers, who, he believed, were fighting for the ideal community, turn out to be little better than robbers. And when not only his political aspirations but also his hope for a happy union with Diotima are frustrated, Hyperion retires from all human society. This solitary resignation does not signify disapproval of the ideal community; it reflects only a regretful acknowledgment that the time for its realization has not yet come. The ideal is not false, but the people are frail. The final passage of the novel is well known; it is a merciless indictment of the German and his barbarism, his narrowness, his tendency to limit his thought to a special profession, his lack of communal spirit. Again it is very illuminating to contrast this critique with Goethe's

ideal of limitation, self-restraint, and bourgeois contentment.
What Hyperion deplored in the German, Empedocles, the
hero of Hölderlin's tragedy, criticizes in the citizen of Agrigentum—the narrowness and specialization of life, the absence of a "great accord." Because he cannot "live in the
universe and love with an ever-present heart, intimately like
a God, and free and all-embracing," because of his ardent
desire for oneness with nature, Empedocles seeks a voluntary
death in the crater of Etna. This at least is the outline of the
tragedy as sketched by Hölderlin in the so-called Frankfort
draft. In a later version (*Der Tod des Empedocles*) it becomes quite clear that Empedocles' death is meant to be not
only a solution of his personal problem but a revelation to the
populace. Empedocles, dying as a prophet, leaves a legacy
to the people of Agrigentum. Only plants and animals are
sufficient unto themselves, he tells them, but death puts an
end to their egocentricity, and they again become one with
nature. So too with the populace; they must voluntarily break
with tradition and custom and, by becoming one with nature,
constitute an ideal community, a brotherhood of thought,
renown, action:

> . . . was ihr geerbt, was ihr erworben,
> Was euch der Väter Mund erzählt, gelehrt,
> Gesetz' und Bräuch', der alten Götter Namen,
> Vergesst es kühn, und hebt, wie Neugeborne,
> Die Augen auf zur göttlichen Natur!
> . . . .
> . . . dann reicht die Hände
> Euch wieder, gebt das Wort und teilt das Gut,
> O dann, ihr Lieben! teilet Tat und Ruhm,
> Wie treue Dioskuren; jeder sei
> Wie alle, wie auf schlanken Säulen ruh
> Auf richt'gen Ordnungen das neue Leben
> Und euren Bund befest'ge das Gesetz.
> Dann, o ihr Genien der wandelnden

Natur! dann ladet euch, ihr heitern,
Das freie Volk zu seinen Festen ein,
Gastfreundlich! fromm! denn liebend gibt
Der Sterbliche vom Besten, schliesst und engt
Den Busen ihm die Knechtschaft nicht—

His message delivered, death becomes imperative for Empedocles: "es muss bei Zeiten weg, durch wen der Geist geredet." In still a third version (*Empedocles auf dem Aetna*) Hölderlin stresses with added intensity the notion that Empedocles is making of himself a propitiatory sacrifice on behalf of mankind. He thus plays a role similar to that of Christ the Savior, the significance of which is recognized by the aged Egyptian Manes:

Der Eine doch, der neue Retter, fasst
Des Himmels Strahlen ruhig auf, und liebend
Nimmt er, was sterblich ist, an seinen Busen,
Und milde wird in ihm der Streit der Welt,
Die Menschen und die Götter söhnt er aus,
Und näher wieder leben sie, wie vormals.
Und dass, wenn er erschienen ist, der Sohn
Nicht grösser, denn die Eltern, sei, und nicht
Der heilge Lebensgeist gefesselt bleibe,
Vergessen über ihm, dem Einzigen,
So lenkt er aus, der Abgott seiner Zeit,
Zerbricht, er selbst, damit durch reine Hand,
Dem Reinen das Notwendige geschehe,
Sein eigen Glück, das ihm zu glücklich ist,
Und gibt, was er besass, dem Element,
Das ihn verherrlichte, geläutert wieder.

Empedocles' act of self-sacrifice may appear to bear a strong resemblance to the kind of renunciation practiced by the heroes of classical tragedy. But again there is a significant difference between Hölderlin and, say, Schiller. In Schiller's world there is an eternal order which the hero recognizes and to which he submits, even to the extent of giving up his life.

This is the classical acceptance of law and order, the classical conformity to the exacting demands of social equilibrium. If a typically Schillerian hero like Max Piccolomini renounces his love and sacrifices his life out of a stern sense of right and duty, he sets an example to others, but he does not vicariously act for them. He shows the way, but all men have to follow the same path for themselves. Another Max Piccolomini would have to make the same sacrifice all over again. It is the very essence of the classical law that it applies to everyone alike and makes universal demands, regardless of the desires of the individual. Schiller's ideal implies not only a single act of sacrifice but a continuity of such renunciation, a constant acknowledgment of superior and super-individual laws. It has aptly been said that the classical hero stands as a typical representative of humanity;[54] and just as his situation is of universal, and not personal and special interest, so his sacrifice represents not his personal fate alone, but, symbolically, the necessity of sacrifice for all humankind.

Empedocles, on the other hand, seeks by his act of sacrifice to found a state in which no further sacrifices will be necessary, an ideal community wherein every individual will be free and happy—the utopian reconciliation of the individual to the whole world. Furthermore, the self-sacrifice of Empedocles is not self-abnegation, self-renunciation, self-conquest, but self-fulfillment. Death is not so much an act of atonement or of tribute to the law, but in Empedocles' own words—a privilege; it is happiness, rebirth, the final ecstasy.[55]

KLEIST

The work of Heinrich von Kleist centers entirely about the conflict between individual and society to a degree perhaps unmatched by the work of any other poet. Even in his first drama, *Die Familie Schroffenstein*, there are indications of his absorption in this problem. It is a drama of the *Romeo*

and Juliet type, in which the lives of two lovers are wrecked
by the mutual hatred of their families. The individual is
thwarted and destroyed by the world he lives in, that is, by
society.[56]

Similarly Kleist's stories depict the destruction and frustration of the individual by the world.[57] In *Die Verlobung in
St. Domingo* two lovers perish through the deadly feud of
their respective races; this is the story of the half-caste
Negress Toni who, in the cruel rising of the black against the
white, lures Gustav into the house of a Negro who plans to
slay him. She falls deeply in love with Gustav, however, and
gives herself to him on the first night. They enter into an
unspoken secret "betrothal." But when Toni, in order to
rescue Gustav, pretends to side with his enemies, he kills her
in the belief that she is unfaithful. When he learns of his
mistake, he kills himself.

Again in *Das Erdbeben in Chile,* two lovers defy society
and fall victims to the hatred and fanaticism of the mob.

So far Kleist seems to be a convinced individualist who
charges human society with the destruction and defeat of the
individual. But his individualism is more profound and more
complicated. Toni and Gustav, for example, do not perish
through external social forces only; if Gustav's belief in Toni
had been stronger, he would have trusted her without fear
of being deceived. Gustav has in fact been unfaithful to his
love, and thus untrue to his inner self. What Kleist preaches
is that the individual must be faithful to himself at all costs,
even in the face of social prejudice and external obstacles.[58]
Only such an interpretation of individualism can supply the
key to an understanding of Kleist's later poems, and notably
to *Penthesilea*.

Penthesilea is queen of the Amazons, who are compelled
by an ancient religious law to acquire their temporary lovers
in war; thus it is not choice but fortuitous accident of battle

which decides with whom an Amazon shall mate. Penthesilea, following natural instinct and personal desire, disregards the command of the law and attempts to capture Achilles. Defeated by him and yet believing that he is her captive, she confesses her love to Achilles. She learns of her defeat, however, when she is freed by her sister warriors. Achilles challenges her to a duel so that he may feign defeat, grant her the triumph of his capture, and subsequently be her lover. This challenge Penthesilea takes as evidence of mockery and contempt. Outraged, she sets out to destroy Achilles with every instrument at her command. After she has killed him, together with her dog she sinks her teeth into his body. But she soon recovers from her madness, denounces the law of the Amazons, and dies by the bare will to die. Again and again the priestess had vainly sought to restrain her by invoking the law from which Penthesilea now finally liberates herself.

This sketchy account does not pretend to convey the strength and quality of the poem, but simply to outline the conflict between the individual and the social standard, in this case between Penthesilea and the law of the Amazons. There is a strong resemblance between the plot of *Penthesilea* and that of Schiller's *Jungfrau von Orleans*. In both cases a woman is called upon to fulfill a prescribed task, on condition that she refrain from allowing personal inclination to interfere. Both transgress this law, it is true, but here the similarity ends. Schiller's heroine attains the classical "Entsagung," renounces her love, bows to the law, and by death expiates her transgression of it. The law is supreme, and the individual must submit. Penthesilea, on the contrary, declares herself free from the law. Her death is no act of atonement or renunciation but a declaration of absolute self-fulfillment, the glorious though belated triumph of the individual. *Penthesilea* and *Die Jungfrau von Orleans* are indeed sharply divergent as to solution, and clearly represent widely different social ideals.

Individualism and self-fulfillment, so forcefully advocated in *Penthesilea*, are glorified also in Kleist's subsequent drama, *Das Käthchen von Heilbronn*. Kleist himself regarded the two plays as complementary. In a dream Käthchen sees a man intended by destiny to be her husband. And when Count Wetter vom Strahl appears at her father's smithy she recognizes him as the man of her dream and trails after him with doglike devotion, despite his apparent desire to be rid of her. She obeys her inclination with no pretense at heroism; she is not to be deterred by any consideration of duty or propriety. She follows her way in a trancelike state. The Count at first resists the "inner call." Though he feels drawn to Käthchen, the Count suppresses his emotion because of the differences in their social rank. Finally, however, he too abandons reflection and reason, responding solely to impulse. He takes a stand for the rights of the individual even before his decision is made unnecessarily easy by the disclosure that Käthchen is the Emperor's natural daughter.

Again in the story of Michael Kohlhaas, the horse dealer, Kleist depicts the most violent clash between the individual and society. Kohlhaas has been unjustly treated: two of his horses have been taken without purchase and crippled by the Junker of Tronka. Kohlhaas is no maniac or fanatic; with admirable patience he investigates the matter and eventually seeks redress in the courts of law. It is only when he finally fails to obtain justice that he resorts to force and revenge. It is true that the two horses do not represent any appreciable loss, but even had they been only two dogs he would have acted in exactly the same way. As an individual, he fights for his individual rights against the State, even to the extent of staking his life and all his property. But it must be remembered that he struggles only against unjust oppression, only against a state which casts him out, robs him of his individuality and thus prevents him from living as a human being. To his wife he says:

Weil ich in einem Lande, liebste Lisbeth, in welchem man mich, in meinen Rechten, nicht schützen will, nicht bleiben mag. Lieber ein Hund sein, wenn ich von Füssen getreten werden soll, als ein Mensch!

And to Luther who seeks to mediate his cause he replies:

Verstossen nenne ich den, dem der Schutz der Gesetze versagt ist! Denn dieses Schutzes, zum Gedeihen meines friedlichen Gewerbes, bedarf ich; ja, er ist es, dessenhalb ich mich, mit dem Kreis dessen, was ich erworben, in diese Gemeinschaft flüchte; und wer ihn mir versagt, der stösst mich zu den Wilden der Einöde hinaus; er gibt mir, wie wollt ihr das leugnen, die Keule, die mich selbst schützt, in die Hand.

Kohlhaas is a law-abiding and dutiful citizen; he fights for his right to be himself, but not for utterly abandoned self-indulgence. In fact he and (so we may now assume) Penthesilea are engaged in a struggle for that ideal community of the romanticists, in which the individual shall be a free, autonomous human being. It would appear, then, that even in these plays and stories which extol "individualism," Kleist is striving for the harmony of individual and society which serves as the theme of his later plays.

A classicist might have treated the subject of Michael Kohlhaas in two ways. Kohlhaas could have fought for the super-individual idea of justice and died for it like a Schillerian hero. Or the story of Kohlhaas could have been made to illustrate the principle that social security and stability must come before individual satisfaction. But Kleist's hero is no idealist; he fights for his right and not for an idea. Nor is the idea of justice or social order urged here as the supreme motivating force.

Under the pressure of political developments and the

Napoleonic Wars, Kleist became a fervent patriot. Nevertheless a close analysis still reveals the same ideal of community, or reconciliation between individual and society, rather than that of an individual entirely submissive to the will of society and its laws.

In *Die Hermannschlacht* the hero goes into battle for the liberation of his people, for national unity, and he even renounces his own independence and ambition for their benefit. Hermann, it is true, submits to his rival, Marbod; but he does not give up every personal desire for the sake of an abstract and binding law. He merely subordinates every other desire to the one he feels to be most urgent and overwhelming, concentrating on one purpose to the exclusion of all others. It is, indeed, the urge within him which he follows without reserve. Hermann makes sacrifices only for the sake of expediency, and his nobility has nothing in common with the self-abnegation which the classicist would regard as man's inescapable duty. *Die Hermannschlacht,* no less than *Penthesilea* or *Michael Kohlhaas,* is a drama of obsession and fanatic self-assertion. Like Penthesilea, Hermann suppresses every emotion, every doubt and every secondary consideration; like Penthesilea, too, he uses every means of combat and summons every thought which might serve to inflame his mind or the minds of his followers. Hermann deliberately chooses to be dishonest, unjust, cruel, sly. Like Kohlhaas, Hermann rejects the notion of fighting for the safety of his possessions or goods; he is willing to lay waste his own lands, to slaughter his own cattle, to burn his own house. His bellicosity is conditioned not by justice or an abstract moral idea, but by his struggle to establish his personal and individual rights, which happen to coincide with those of his people. He wants to regain for his people and for himself the right to be their own sovereign selves, to lead their own individual lives; and he accuses the Romans of criminal disregard for the individuality, dignity, and humanity of the German people:

HERMANN: Für wen erschaffen war die Welt als Rom?
  Nimmt August nicht dem Elephanten
  Das Elfenbein, das Öl der Bisamkatze,
  Dem Panthertier das Fell, dem Wurm die Seide?
  Was soll der Deutsche hier zum voraus haben?
THUSNELDA (sieht ihn an): Was wir zum voraus sollen—?
HERMANN: Allerdings.
THUSNELDA: Dass du verderben müsstest mit Vernünfteln!
  Das sind ja Tiere, Querkopf, der du bist,
  Und keine Menschen!
HERMANN: Menschen! Ja, mein Thuschen,
  Was ist der Deutsche in der Römer Augen?
THUSNELDA: Nun, doch kein Tier, hoff' ich—?
HERMANN: Was?—Eine Bestie,
  Die auf vier Füssen in den Wäldern läuft!
  Ein Tier, das, wo der Jäger es erschaut,
  Just einen Pfeilschuss wert, mehr nicht,
  Und ausgeweidet und gepelzt dann wird!

Once again it is interesting to contrast Kleist with Schiller. Schiller's patriotism means discipline, and it implies ethical and moral service for a super-individual, external, transcendent idea; Schiller's "Vaterlandsgefühl" deals with so abstract a morality that he can glorify the struggle for freedom and justice in terms of French and Swiss history. But with Kleist the question whether Hermann's cause is just or good has no significance. Hermann subscribes to no moral law; he follows his own instinct, his own passion. His patriotism is a sensation of rapture and frenzy, whereas that of Wilhelm Tell is a righteous and moral sentiment, reflecting dispassionate and sober recognition of an exacting duty. Both Wilhelm Tell and Joan of Arc fulfill their missions as such, without allowing any personal motives to interfere and even by conquering their own natural inclinations. Hermann, on the contrary, makes no attempt at self-restraint. For him the task is not one of "duty" in response to external command, but of self-fulfillment which his very nature demands. No Schillerian hero could ever have announced that good and noble enemies are more to be hated than evil ones. Hermann, however, curses the good Romans because the consideration of their virtue might reflect his rage and thus make him waver in his fidelity. Like Kohlhaas, like Penthesilea, like Käthchen, Hermann is called upon steadfastly to follow his nature and his instinct. No emotion must be permitted to deter him from "being himself."

Our particular approach has perhaps led us to discern still more profound and complex problems in Kleist's patriotic drama, and the interpretation presented here must make no claim to finality. But—and this of course is a simplification—we may fairly say that Hermann does not renounce his individuality for the sake of an order imposed by classical society; instead he achieves self-fulfillment within the romantic community.

The harmonious reconciliation between the individual and the state serves also as the theme of Kleist's last drama, *Prinz Friedrich von Homburg*. In the opening scene the prince is observed walking in his sleep by the Elector, Natalie, and others. When the prince awakes, he finds a glove in his hand. The next day, as he and the other officers gather in the palace to receive their orders for battle, the prince learns that the glove belongs to Natalie, his beloved. Carried away by his hope and confidence, the prince listens only half-heartedly to the orders given him. Thus in the battle, although he wins a decisive victory, he acts contrary to the strict command he has received. He is arrested, brought before a court-martial, and sentenced to death. At first the prince believes that his uncle, the Elector, is only complying with the letter of the law, and intends to commute the sentence, and it is not until he witnesses the actual preparation for his execution and sees his open grave that he realizes the gravity of his plight. Now he breaks down completely and begs for life, no matter how ignoble. He renounces his love for Natalie, his honor, indeed everything but life itself. When the Elector hears of the prince's collapse, he sends a message to him, granting his freedom if he considers the sentence unjust. By this time, however, the prince has recovered somewhat. When his fellow officers present a petition to the Elector and even threaten rebellion if the prince is not released, the Elector can look to the prisoner himself for justification of the sentence. The prince has recognized his wrongdoing and is prepared to atone for it with his death:

> Es ist mein unbeugsamer Wille!
> Ich will das heilige Gesetz des Kriegs,
> Das ich verletzt' im Angesicht des Heers,
> Durch einen freien Tod verherrlichen!
> Was kann der Sieg euch, meine Brüder, gelten,
> Der eine, dürftige, den ich vielleicht
> Dem Wrangel noch entreisse, dem Triumph
> Verglichen über den verderblichsten
> Der Feind' in uns, den Trotz, den Übermut,
> Errungen glorreich morgen?

Superficially this might appear to be a classical drama of self-conquest, with the hero renouncing his individuality and surrendering to the supreme law. And it must be admitted that in every respect this is Kleist's most classical, or better, classicist, drama. Yet the more profound implications of this play are by no means purely classical. Indeed scholars have sought to present a satisfactory interpretation of its underlying significance. Thus far, there are three outstanding explanations. According to the first, the play shows that personal and individual initiative triumphs over the rigidity of the abstract law. The second holds that it represents the triumph of a law which is sacred and superior to the individual. The third interpretation, as might be expected, is based upon the assumption that Kleist has effected a compromise between the first two.[59] As in many controversies of this nature, the compromise seems the most satisfactory.

Here again we have the romantic idea of a community to which the individual belongs by virtue of his very individuality. If the prince is moved to surrender to the law, the Elector either has always recognized the value of individual initiative or has just been converted to this point of view.[60] And we are left with the conviction that Kottwitz, one of the prince's fellow officers, speaks to the point when he says that he does not shed his blood for fame or earthly advantage, but because it is his nature to do so; whereas the blind and rigid law would make soldiers into slaves and mere automatons:

> Herr, das Gesetz, das höchste, oberste,
> Das wirken soll, in deiner Feldherrn Brust,
> Das ist der Buchstab deines Willens nicht;
> Das ist das Vaterland, das ist die Krone,
> Das bist du selber, dessen Haupt sie trägt.
> Was kümmert dich, ich bitte dich, die Regel,
> Nach der der Feind sich schlägt: wenn er nur nieder
> Vor dir, mit allen seinen Fahnen, sinkt?
> Die Regel, die ihn schlägt, das ist die höchste!
> Willst du das Heer, das glühend an dir hängt,
> Zu einem Werkzeug machen, gleich dem Schwerte,
> Das tot in deinem goldnen Gürtel ruht?
> Der ärmste Geist, der, in den Sternen fremd,
> Zuerst solch eine Lehre gab! Die schlechte,
> Kurzsicht'ge Staatskunst, die um eines Falles,
> Da die Empfindung sich verderblich zeigt,
> Zehn andere vergisst, im Lauf der Dinge,
> Da die Empfindung einzig retten kann!
> Schütt' ich mein Blut dir, an dem Tag der Schlacht,
> Für Sold, sei's Geld, sei's Ehre, in den Staub?
> Behüte Gott! Dazu ist es zu gut!
> Was, meine Lust hab', meine Freude ich,
> Frei und für mich, im Stillen, unabhängig,
> An deiner Trefflichkeit und Herrlichkeit!

It is not the state as oppressor of the individual which triumphs in the play, but the community of free human beings. When he determines to expiate his offence the prince does not renounce his real nature; for in giving himself up he finds himself. His disobedience is a mistake for which he is only partly responsible and which, at bottom, is not consistent with his true self. The prince can do what neither Penthesilea, nor Kohlhaas, nor Käthchen, nor Hermann could do—he can acknowledge his wrong—because by this avowal he commits no betrayal of his genius, his mission, or his inner voice. The theme is not self-conquest but self-discovery.

We have endeavored in the foregoing discussion to show that the gulf between Kleist's early poems and his later work is not unbridgeable, and to this end have emphasized the continuity of thought from *Penthesilea* to *Die Hermannschlacht*, from *Kohlhaas* to *Prinz Friedrich von Homburg*. The fundamental problem in all these dramas remains the relationship between the individual and society; the constant ideal is the reconciliation of the two within the community. But there is nevertheless a clearly perceptible evolution in Kleist's work, from emphasis upon the individualistic aspect to that upon the more collectivistic. Kleist wrestles with the problem, but never solves it to his permanent satisfaction. Again and again he starts afresh, reveals new aspects, tries a new solution, and remains tormented by the task he has set himself. The very fact that he inevitably returns to the problem, that he is always absorbed by it, not as conscious or theoretical doctrine, but as his underlying "Weltanschauung," indicates that neither classical self-denial nor Sturm-und-Drang individualism can provide the answer for him.

Although Kleist bears some relationship to members of one or the other romantic school, he cannot be said to belong to a romantic school in the narrower sense of the term. More broadly, however, it is admissible to call him a romanticist, much as in the case of Hölderlin. Kleist's treatment of the position of the individual within society, within the world,

seems indeed to justify such a classification, although it may
well be remembered that labels are relatively unimportant.

ARNIM

Whereas Kleist gradually shifted his emphasis from the individual aspect of "community" to the collective one, Achim
von Arnim was always inclined to stress the collective and
communal most strongly. There are several reasons for Arnim's attitude, the most significant being the fact that he
came of the North German gentry and had a stern Protestant
background. It is not surprising, therefore, that he found
rigidity and discipline more to his taste than subjectivism
and individualism. Arnim, unlike Kleist, never broke deci-
sively with aristocratic tradition.

Under the influence of Goethe's *Wahlverwandtschaften*
Arnim wrote a novel about marriage which superficially
seems to endorse Goethe's stand, to glorify subordination and
renunciation. *Armut, Reichtum, Schuld und Busse der Gräfin
Dolores* is a history of adultery and penitence. Count P. is a
waster who, after squandering his fortune, deserts his two
daughters. The girls, Dolores and Klelia, are left in extreme
poverty. And Dolores, who is extravagant, fond of luxury
and amusement, rather heartless and superficial, marries
Count Karl not so much because she loves him, but because
the arrangement promises a life of ease and comfort. Klelia,
more honest, more serious, more pious, accompanies an aunt
to Sicily and eventually marries a Duke whom she believes
worthy not only of her love but also of her respect. Posing
as a friend of the Duke (while actually he is the Duke himself in disguise) the Marquis of D. visits Dolores and Karl
and seduces Dolores. He imposes on her vanity and her religious sentiments so that she yields to him against her will
and virtually in a state of trance. When Karl discovers his
wife's infidelity he plans to make her the murderess of his

body as well as of his honor and happiness. He arranges matters so that during a shooting competition she pulls the trigger of a rifle pointed toward his heart. But he is miraculously saved. Dolores confesses her sin and becomes a completely changed person. Karl sees in his salvation a sign of God, and when he meets Dolores on a pilgrimage, he finally forgives her. For the rest of her life Dolores is a most unselfish wife and mother. She and Karl leave the scene of their unhappy memories and go to live with Klelia in Sicily, and there Dolores spends long years of self-sacrificial devotion to her growing family. Various circumstances lead also to the arrival in Sicily of the Princess, who falls vainly in love with Karl. He fails not only to return her love, but even to realize that she has conceived a passion for him. But everything combines to confirm Dolores in her opinion that Karl loves the Princess, and she imagines it to be her duty to give him his freedom, to atone for her previous sin by renunciation. The anguish which leads her to this decision and the decision itself bring her to her deathbed. Karl arrives too late to clear up the misunderstanding. Dolores dies on the fourteenth anniversary of the day on which she had violated her sacred vow to God and to her husband.

In contrast to his wife, who in the beginning was vain and designing, Karl is a man of the world, purposeful, energetic, idealistic. He takes an interest in his estates and in the education of his subjects, resembling in this respect many of Goethe's characters, notably Eduard, or the captain of the *Wahlverwandtschaften*. But what distinguishes him fundamentally from the active and socially minded hero of the last act of *Faust* or from the Wilhelm Meister of the *Wanderjahre*, is the complete absence of any need for renunciation on his part. Faust and Meister arrive at a satisfactory interpretation of life only after painful, almost suicidal self-conquest, just as Goethe himself has done in assuming the post

of Minister at Weimar, and indeed just as Goethe's classicism
had developed in reaction to his Sturm-und-Drang youth.

There is also a remarkable difference in the problem of
marriage as treated in *Dolores* and in the *Wahlverwandtschaften*. Dolores is seduced and then abandoned by her seducer. Her adultery is to be attributed to her weakness and
vanity; it is, in a sense, a misunderstanding, an error, for she
does not love her seducer. And her atonement is not so much
an act of penance and self-denial as a discovery of her "true"
self. The following passage is particularly interesting, occur-
ring as it does at the stage of the novel where Dolores takes
her first steps on the downward path:

Wir, die wir den Ausgang kennen, wünschen, sie wäre dem Winke
ihrer Natur gefolgt, der Natur, die sich in ihrer Sehnsucht und
Laune selten ungestraft widersprechen lässt, denn sie allein weiss,
was sie will, wir aber wollen, was wir nicht wissen.

Dolores' sin is a departure from nature. The leading characters in the *Wahlverwandtschaften*, on the other hand, are
shaken profoundly by passion, and it is only through the
most mortifying self-denial, virtually through an amputation
of part of the living body, that they achieve submission to
law and morality. It is interesting here to recall the famous
passage in the *Wahlverwandtschaften* wherein Eduard, Charlotte, and the captain discuss the affinities between certain
chemical elements and how the closest union of two elements
may be destroyed by a third. Charlotte protests against the
technical term "Wahlverwandtschaft" because of its impli-
cation that there is a choice; nature, destiny, necessity, are
the motivating forces. Once the elements are juxtaposed so
that they can exercise their attraction on each other there
is no way out: "Dann gnade ihnen Gott!" In the same way
the characters themselves are pushed, compelled, predestined.
Their passion is as inevitable, indeed as necessary as the
movement of the stars; and their renunciation is suicidal in

a deeper sense; for only by killing their own true selves can they find peace. As if to emphasize this almost fatalistic necessity, Goethe introduces certain ominous coincidences—Ottilie's birthday falls on the anniversary of the day when Eduard planted his sycamore trees; a miraculously preserved wine glass bears the initials E (Eduard) and O (Ottilie), etc.[61] In fact, Goethe places so much emphasis upon the inevitability of his characters' several tragedies that Eichendorff was moved to call the novel an apology for adultery.[62] There is no such inevitable destiny against which Dolores must take a heroic stand; nor does she have to stifle a consuming passion. Goethe subordinates his characters, at the cost of their individuality, to the law of society, while Arnim prefers that Dolores, as an individual, should find her place within the community.

And if in the end there is a sort of classical renunciation on the part of Dolores, it is again the result of a misunderstanding, for she takes this step not because she thinks Karl is in the right but simply because she believes that by her earlier sin she has lost the privilege of claiming what is hers. It is a lack of self-confidence and a gnawing conscience, rather than a moral conviction which causes her to make the sacrifice; and she makes it not to uphold the law, but on the contrary to assist Karl to evade the law. Her sacrifice is thus motivated by her desire to punish herself, and not by submission to any eternal, super-individual law. If any comparison is to be made between a character in *Dolores* and one in *Die Wahlverwandtschaften*, then only the Princess can be so viewed, for she is consumed by a passion which finally destroys her; but even she fails to achieve purification through "Entsagung."

What Arnim seeks is not the objective, abstract, and rational order; not society, but comradeship, brotherhood, community—a subjective "living-for-each-other." This motive becomes even clearer in his great historical novel, *Die Kronenwächter,* which Arnim has invested with depth and richness of color by presenting a wealth of detail and incident and by introducing old superstitions and other elements of German folk-lore. However, only the first part of the novel, dealing with "Berthold's first and second life," is finished. The existing drafts and fragments of the second part seem to belong to an earlier stage of Arnim's thought, but permit nevertheless a reconstruction of the broad outlines of the plot.[63]

As in *Wilhelm Meister,* there is a secret society which governs the life and destiny of those it elects to membership. In *Wilhelm Meister* it was the Society of the Tower; in *Die Kronenwächter* it is the clique of the guardians who, in a mysterious castle, watch over the Hohenstaufen crown. Berthold, a descendant of the imperial Hohenstaufen family, grows up under such secret guardianship. At the beginning he is taken by them to Martin, the watchman on the Weibling tower. Martin is eventually killed by the "guardians" when he is about to betray their secret. At various stages in the novel Arnim describes the ruthless cruelty of the "guardians," who separate lovers, punish with death those who disobey, kidnap children, and commit similar atrocities. Berthold first becomes a scribe, then a wealthy merchant and manufacturer, and finally mayor of his town. But he is sickly, and Faust gives him another lease of life by transfusing into his veins the blood of Anton, another Hohenstaufen. Thus Berthold begins his second life, which, under the direction of the "guardians" is partly devoted to an abortive attempt to restore the Hohenstaufen family to the throne. Berthold dies when Anton is wounded and bleeding, for it is Anton's blood which hitherto has kept him alive. Anton marries Berthold's wife who has been drawn to him by the magic of the blood-spell. After many wanderings and adventures, Anton reaches the castle of the guardians and destroys it. The sinister power of the "Kronenwächter" is thus broken, and Germany can now be reborn.

The "guardians" are despots and tyrants, representing the notion of strict subordination and blind obedience. Their power is frightful and sinister, their ideals are outmoded and reactionary. They suppress ruthlessly the feelings and inclinations of the individual, so that service with them is even more difficult than that imposed by a religious order, and the discipline is as rigid as that prevailing in a military camp. At one point a father exclaims, after the death of his daughter: "For years I have guarded a crown I will never wear, and I have permitted my child, whom my wife has borne with love and pain, to stray." Those whom the guardians elect as heirs to the throne are caught like flies in a spider's web. It is this lack of freedom, this self-abnegation, this severity with which orders are enforced and disobedience is punished—it is this very mechanism, set up to unite Germany and to impose a social order upon her, which must be overcome and defeated before the true community of free individuals can emerge. Thus the significance and projected ending of the novel seem unequivocal—the castle and the guardians must be destroyed before the brotherhood of all Germany can be established.

The relation between the individual and society for Arnim, as for Kleist, Novalis, and other romanticists, is a troublesome problem, an ever-present source of disquiet in the author's mind, whereas the classicist has arrived at a solution, has settled the problem perhaps at the cost of resignation and self-renunciation, but has nevertheless gained, by his decision, a relatively safe and assured position. For Goethe, and even more for Schiller, the supremacy of the law and the value of the act of sacrifice and self-denial are beyond cavil. Schiller's plays all serve to underline this conviction. For the romanticist, on the other hand, the position of the individual within society always remains something of a problem because—since he cannot conceive of one as superior or inferior to the other—he must seek constantly to reconcile them. Thus the romanticists may be said to have reopened the proceedings in a case which the classicists thought they had closed.

"POLITISCHE ROMANTIK"

Like the Stürmer-und-Dränger, the romanticists have a predilection for tales of the type of *Faust* and *Fortunatus*—of the hero who sells his soul in order to experience a complete life. But the romantic hero is seldom a titanic rebel, a Prometheus or a Faust, who defies divine as well as satanic power to the very end and who, in order to still his desires, would turn both society and the world upside down. Klinger's Faust, as we have seen, neither repents nor reforms. Even in the grip of Satan he remains defiant and rebellious.

The romanticist Chamisso, however, causes his *Peter Schlemihl* to regret his transaction with the devil. Schlemihl had entered into the contract without realizing what he was doing, and he soon learns that the ideal is to live within the community. He suffers from his abnormality and isolation; and Chamisso, an exile himself, may have been particularly inclined to sympathize with the lonely outcast. Schlemihl longs to have a shadow. And the shadow, as Thomas Mann has interpreted the story in his *Bemühungen*, means respectability as a member of the human community: "Der Schatten ist im "Peter Schlemihl" zum Symbol aller bürgerlichen Solidität und menschlichen Zugehörigkeit geworden."

Individualism and collectivism, as we have observed, are the two interdependent and constituent aspects of romantic community. Tieck in *Sternbald* and *Lovell*, Brentano in *Godwi*, Schlegel in *Lucinde*, all place more stress on the individualistic aspect, while Arnim and Chamisso tend to emphasize the communal. This in general was the course of development from early to later romanticism. The individualistic aspect of community gradually gives way to the collectivistic and ultimately leads to emphatic affirmation of the idea of "state." But even then, the state, it should be noted, stands for the absolute consummation of the individual and not for a body of abstract regulations which bind and strangle him.

It is this marked interest in the communal aspect which accounts also for the conversion of many romanticists to Catholicism, for their patriotism and political conservatism, and even for their subservience to the reactionary Metternich. They have come to look upon the Catholic Church and the feudal state as two examples of "community," and for this reason they romanticize the Middle Ages. Again it is well to remember that this final development does not constitute a break with early romanticism, but merely indicates a shift of stress. Wackenroder and Tieck had already directed attention to the Middle Ages and to Catholicism, and had reawakened interest in national art and history. As early as 1806, this patriotic and antiquarian interest led to the publication by Arnim and Brentano of *Des Knaben Wunderhorn*. And Novalis' *Die Christenheit oder Europa* had been written back in 1799.

Eventually, romanticism turned from nostalgia for the golden age to political philosophy and theoretical tracts on state and government. Social ideals, now subject to systematic formulation, were therefore bound to become more and more realistic. This so-called "Politische Romantik" is discussed intensively at the present time, especially by such scholars as Schmitt and Kluckhohn.[64] The romantic political theorists—Novalis, Schlegel, and especially Adam Müller—are acclaimed today as the prophets of dictatorship and the totalitarian state.

Since this study is limited to the ideals expressed in imaginative literature, we shall refer here only briefly to political romanticism, which belongs more properly to the sphere of economists and politicians than to that of literary historians. It seems clear that the state advocated by the romanticists is the very embodiment of community—a harmonious "organism," of which all parts are bound together in mutual service. A part severed from the whole would die, and a desire to live within the community is therefore not renunciation but self-fulfillment. Schleiermacher, in his *Monologen,* holds that the state is destined to give man the highest degree of life: "ihm den höchsten Grad des Lebens zu gewähren."

Novalis, in the poems we have already discussed, dreamed of a time when the individual would live in harmonious accord with all other men, so that his individuality would receive added strength from the relationship:

> Alles muss in einander greifen,
> Eins durch das andre gedeihn und reifen;
> Jedes in allen dar sich stellt,
> Indem es sich mit ihnen vermischet
> Und gierig in ihre Tiefe fällt,
> Sein eigentümliches Wesen erfrischet
> Und tausend neue Gedanken erhält.

These ideas he formulated also theoretically in a collection of aphorisms called *Glauben und Liebe* (1798) and in the essay *Die Christenheit oder Europa* (1799). Here he advocates a monarchical system, emphasizes the collective aspect of the state, and praises the medieval hierarchy, thus heralding the later development of romantic political thought.

Although Hölderlin[50] disparages the state while Novalis eulogizes it, both can nevertheless share the same social ideal because each interprets the term "state" in a different manner. Hölderlin maintains that the state is based on the extinction of the individual and is therefore opposed to his ideal of community. For Novalis, the state is in fact a community in which man's individuality finds most complete expression. And according to the theories of the political romanticists, the state is a product of historic development and therefore the natural and proper "setting" for the life of the nation as a whole and of its individual members. It is this "Organic State" which is idealized by Adam Müller and later by Hegel.

Adam Müller, it is true, pleads for a strong state. But he expressly insists that the state should allow free development to every individual:[65]

Der Staat verstatte dem Menschen das zu sein und ohne Ende immer mehr zu werden, was er seiner eigentümlichen Natur und seinem individuellen Wachstum nach sein kann.

Inequalities among men, differences of sex, age, and social class, are profoundly necessary to Müller's state, just as discrete and individual parts are indispensable to an organism. Müller cannot conceive of a state in which men would no longer be different, but would conform to a single ideal. Nor is "law" of a higher order than the individual and imposed alike upon all men from without, as the classicist maintained; It is merely the instrument whereby the harmony of conflicting individual interests is achieved. Müller asserts that there can be no law unless there are individuals who follow the dictates of their particular nature. And the more intransigent every individual is in asserting his rights and pressing his claims, the more perfect will the law be:[66]

Je mehr der einzelne Anspruch des Bürgers die Freiheit hat, gegen einen entgegengesetzten eben so freien Anspruch eines andern Bürgers sich geltend zu machen: um so mehr wird das Gesetz, welches diese gegenseitigen Ansprüche regulieren soll, ausgeschliffen und vollendet werden. Je lebhafter und je vielseitiger der Streit ist, den die beiden Parteien vor Gericht führen; je mehr jede Partei zu Worte kommt: um so gediegner, lebendiger und ideenhafter wird der Urteilsspruch ausfallen können.

The state, like the law, has arisen out of the needs and desires of its members, and hence is adapted to their requirements. Müller's state is a vital, flexible organism.[67]

Er (der Staat) ist die innige Verbindung der gesamten physischen und geistigen Bedürfnisse, des gesamten physischen und geistigen Reichtums, des gesamten innern und äussern Lebens einer Nation, zu einem grossen, energischen, unendlich bewegten und lebendigen Ganzen.

Man, in the classical view, had free will; he could elect renunciation and subordination to the law. Müller, on the other hand, maintains that man can no more choose to live outside the community than he can choose to live outside the earth itself. To live within the community is man's inescapable condition.

To the Stürmer-und-Dränger, the man of genius stood apart from society, towering above it in titanic greatness. To the romanticist, however, the great man is the product of his time, of his country, of his surroundings; he is historically conditioned, developing against a specific background and within a particular community. The great man is no longer regarded as isolated, but as molded by the period in which he lives, his contemporaries, his immediate environment. The romantic tendency to place the individual within a wider context had already been suggested by Herder. Today it is generally agreed that the current movement in modern humanities ("Geisteswissenschaften") for a history which eschews the individual as such and presents a synthetic view in which he is studied in a broader context, goes back ultimately to romanticism.

The romantic ideal of "community" could develop into both the reactionary glorification of the absolute state, and the revolutionary and liberal attitude of the French romanticists.

NOTES AND REFERENCES

1. Our analysis does not do justice to Lessing's play. For Emilia Galotti is not only the victim of forces outside herself; she also experiences within herself the conflict between her inclination toward the prince and her sense of honor. Her death saved her from herself more than from the prince. Since we are concerned with Lessing's social ideal, however, we have taken the liberty of simplifying the argument.

2. *Deutsche Literaturdenkmale des 18. und 19. Jahrhunderts,* hrsg. v. Seuffert etc., XXIII, 302.

3. *Der junge Goethe,* ed. M. Morris, Leipzig, 1909–12, V, 100.

4. We find the same self-assurance in Goethe's "An Schwager Kronos," wherein death is regarded as a triumphant entry into Hades.

5. *Dichtungen,* ed. H. Hettner, Leipzig, 1868 (Bibl. d. dt. Nat.-lit. d. 18. u. 19. Jhs.), I, 126.

6. Compare G. Stockmeyer, *Soziale Probleme im Drama des Sturm-und-Dranges,* Frankf. a. M., 1922 (Dt. Forschungen, hrsg. v. Panzer u. Petersen, Vol. 5).

7. Carlton J. H. Hayes, "Contributions of Herder to the doctrine of nationalism," *American Hist. Rev.* XXXII (1927), 719ff.; R. R. Ergang, *Herder and the Foundations of German Nationalism,* New York, 1931; K. S. Pinson, *Pietism as a Factor in the Rise of German Nationalism,* New York, 1934.

8. Fritz Strich, *Deutsche Klassik und Romantik,* p. 391.

9. Georg Simmel, *Goethe,* Leipzig, 1913, p. 142f. Simmel speaks of "formale Individualität" and "quantitative Individualität." Compare also Simmel, *Soziologie,* 2. Aufl., München, 1922, p. 541f.

10. Strich in *Deutsche Vierteljahrschrift f. Litw. u. Geistesgesch.,* I, 591; reprinted in Strich, *Dichtung und Zivilisation,* München, 1928, p. 35.

11. Compare, for example, Richard Alewyn, *Johann Beer,* Leip-

zig, 1932 (Palästra CLXXXI), p. 169f., or Karl Vietor, *Probleme der deutschen Barockliteratur*, Leipzig, 1928, p. 13.

12. F. Strich, *Dt. Klassik u. Romantik*, p. 91: "Die klassische Entäusserung war die Entäusserung des zeitlichen Menschen zur zeitlosen Gattung oder Idee des Menschentums. Diese verwirklicht sich in der geschlossenen, kosmischen, vollendeten Form der Persönlichkeit."

13. Jubiläums-Ausgabe, XXXIV, 11ff.

14. H. A. Korff, *Geist der Goethezeit*, II, 362ff. It should be noted here that the romanticist admired deeply both *Hermann und Dorothea* and *Wilhelm Meister*. A. W. Schlegel, in his essay on *Hermann und Dorothea*, praises the epic poise, the calm, balanced narrative, the impartiality and aloofness of the poet ("Absonderungsvermögen") which impart order and measure to the poem. He also stresses the "humanizing" treatment of the plot. All these are typically classical qualities which the romanticist approves. But it seems likely that the social tendency struck most romanticists as Philistine.

15. Instead of having a long list of citations, the reader is referred to the heading, "Entsagung," in the index of the "Jubiläums-Ausgabe."

16. Jub.-Ausg., XXVIII, 251.

17. *Ibid.*, XI, 87.

18. *Ibid.*, XI, 125.

19. *Ibid.*, XVIII, 254.

20. *Ibid.*, XVIII, 255.

21. *Ibid.*, XVIII, 296.

22. *Ibid.*, XVIII, 297.

23. *Ibid.*, XVIII, 150.

24. *Ibid.*, XVIII, 152.

25. Although the main development is toward social adaptation and disciplined activity, Wilhelm's relation to women is strongly reminiscent of the Sturm-und-Drang attitude. With Marianne, the Countess, Mignon, and probably even Philine, he behaves in a manner which is far from praiseworthy. Wilhelm, and Lothario as well, still act on the principle that a man has the right to sacri-

fice others to his genius. There is, however, a difference between this attitude and the self-assertion typical of the Sturm-und-Drang.

26. Jub.-Ausg., XVIII, 326.

27. *Ibid.*, XVIII, 328.

28. *Ibid.*, XVIII, 14.

29. *Ibid.*, XIX, 39.

30. *Ibid.*, XIX, 171.

31. Compare Karl Muthesius, *Goethe und das Handwerk*, Leipzig, 1927.

32. W. Wittich, "Der soziale Gehalt in Goethes Roman 'W. M. L.'," in *Hauptprobleme der Soziologie: Erinnerungsgabe für Max Weber*, München u. Leipzig, 1923, II, 277ff.; G. Radbruch, "W. M.'s sozialpolitische Sendung," in *Logos* VIII (1920), 152ff. Less valuable for this particular study is W. Schütz, *Die Staatsidee des W. M.*, Heilbronn a. N., 1935, and Werner Richter, *Goethe und der Staat* (Kieler Vorträge gehalten im Wissenschaftlichen Klub des Instituts für Weltwirtschaft u. Seeverkehr a. d. Univ. Kiel, hrsg. v. . . . Bernhard Harms, 36), Jena, 1932.

33. Jub.-Ausg., XXIX, 21.

34. Mention should be made, however, of the passage in *Die Wanderjahre* (II, 2) in which Goethe states that it is a principle of the "Pädagogische Provinz" *not* to allow children to wear uniform.

35. Goethe's "Römische Elegien" have often been so interpreted as to contradict a rigid view of marriage. But Korff, op. cit. p. 326, refutes this interpretation conclusively.

36. Jub.-Ausg., XII, 366.

37. The development of Faust, as outlined above, corresponds to the sequence of the scenes in the finished tragedy. But the scenes and acts were not written by Goethe in this order; the fourth act, for example, was written later than the fifth.

38. *Dichtung und Wahrheit*, Book 16.

39. *Caroline, Briefe aus der Frühromantik*, nach Georg Waitz vermehrt, hrsg. v. E. Schmidt, Leipzig, 1913, I, 570.

40. Ferdinand Tönnies, *Gemeinschaft und Gesellschaft*, 6. u.

7. Aufl., Berlin, 1925. Compare also Tönnies in *Handwörterbuch der Soziologie*, ed. A. Vierkandt, Stuttgart, 1931, and *Walter Strich, Der irrationale Mensch*, Berlin, 1928, p. 355ff.

41. F. Strich, *Dt. Klassik und Romantik*, p. 94; Paul Kluckhohn, *Persönlichkeit und Gemeinschaft*, p. 15.

42. For an exhaustive analysis, see Paul Kluckhohn, *Die Auffassung der Liebe in der Literatur des 18. Jahrhunderts und in der deutschen Romantik*, Halle, 1922. For the whole chapter, compare also Fritz Lübbe, *Die Wendung vom Individualismus zur sozialen Gemeinschaft im romantischen Roman* (Literatur und Seele etc., ed. Fritz Brüggemann, Band 2), Berlin, 1931.

43. *Werke*, ed. Kluckhohn und Samuel, III, 313.

44. For a considered interpretation, see Kluckhohn's introduction to the edition cited above.

45. Compare also L. v. Pigenot, *Hölderlin*, München, 1923, p. 132f.

46. Compare W. Willige, "Deutschland, Hellas und Hölderlin," *Zeitschrift für Deutschkunde*, XLI (1927), 355ff.

47. Ludwig Strauss, "Natur und Gemeinschaft, Stücke einer Hölderlinbiographie." *Die Kreatur* II (1927–28), 295ff.; L. Strauss, *Das Problem der Gemeinschaft in Hölderlins Hyperion* (Von Dt. Poeterey 15), Leipzig, 1933.

48. Julius Petersen, "Das goldene Zeitalter bei den Romantikern," in *Die Ernte, Festschr. f. Muncker*, Halle, 1926.

49. Werke, ed. Hellingrath, II, 546. Compare also the preface to the so-called Thalia-Fragment.

50. Edition cited, p. 121f.

51. *Ibid.*, p. 197.

52. *Ibid.*, p. 183ff.

53. For example, Goethe, in the paragraph, "Antikes," of *Winckelmann und sein Jahrhundert*, Jub.-Ausg., XXXIV, 11f.

54. Strich, *Deutsche Klassik und Romantik*, p. 20: "Denn Mensch sein heisst: das Urbild des Menschentums, das zeitlose Wesen der menschlichen Gattung in sich zu verwirklichen und sich zum symbolischen Repräsentanten der ewigen Menschheit zu erhöhen."

55. From the rather difficult and often elusive theoretical treatise on Empedocles (*Grund zum Empedokles*) we can appreciate Hölderlin's absorption in the problem of reconciling the individual with mankind as a whole.

56. Kurt Allert, *Einzelmensch und Gemeinschaft bei H. v. K.*, Königsberger phil. Diss., 1925 (Typescript only).

57. B. Payr, "Der Sinn der Novellen K.s.," *Herrig's Arch.*, CLXVI, 380ff. The thesis that K.'s stories show the individual in a world of error, misunderstanding, and confusion, is by no means so new as the author seems to think.

58. Hermann Pongs, "Möglichkeiten des Tragischen in der Novelle," *Jahrbuch d. Kleist-Ges.*, XIII–XIV (1932), 38ff. For the entire chapter on Kleist, see also G. Fricke, *Gefühl und Schicksal bei K.* (Neue Forschung, ed. Hecht u. Naumann, 3), Berlin, 1929.

59. Horst Engert "Persönlichkeit und Gemeinschaft in K.'s Drama 'Prinz Friedrich von Homburg'," *Jahrbuch der Kleist-Gesellschaft*, VII–VIII (1925–26), p. 1ff.

60. Whether the character of the Elector is constant throughout the play, or whether he, too, undergoes a change corresponding, but contrary, to that of the prince, is one of the moot controversies in the interpretation of the play. But whatever his development, he does meet the prince halfway, and a compromise is finally reached between the individual and society. This compromise is basic to the idea of "community."

61. For Goethe, destiny can and must be overcome by man. It makes man's striving and sacrifices more difficult but at the same time more valuable; whereas, for the writers of the romantic "Schicksalstragödie," man was an important puppet of destiny.

62. Eichendorff, *Der dt. Roman des 18. Jhs. i. s. Verh. z. Christentum*, Leipzig, 1851, p. 98f.

63. For an interpretation of *Die Kronenwächter*, see J. Nadler, *Die Berliner Romantik*, Berlin, 1921.

64. Only a small selection from the vast literature on the subject could be given in the bibliography. The reader will find it useful to examine the survey of literature on "Neuere Staatsan-

schauung," published regularly in *Jahresberichte für deutsche Geschichte*.

65. Quoted by Kluckhohn, *Persönlichkeit und Gemeinschaft*, p. 75.

66. Bülow's edition, p. 73.

67. *Ibid.*, p. 28.

SELECTED BIBLIOGRAPHY

EDITIONS or books quoted in the notes with reference to one special point, are given there with all the bibliographical data and are not repeated here.

I. EDITIONS

Goethe, Sämtliche Werke, Jubiläums-Ausgabe in 40 Bänden und Registerband. Herausgegeben von E. v. d. Hellen. Stuttgart, 1902–12.

Hölderlin, Sämtliche Werke, Historisch-kritische Ausgabe begonnen durch N. v. Hellingrath, fortgeführt durch F. Seebass und L. v. Pigenot. 6 Bände. München (later Berlin), 1913–23.

Novalis, Schriften, im Verein mit R. Samuel herausgegeben von P. Kluckhohn. 4 Bände. Leipzig [1928].

Müller, Adam, Vom Geiste der Gemeinschaft, "Elemente der Staatskunst" und "Theorie des Geldes" zusammengefasst und eingeleitet von F. Bülow (Kröners Taschenausgaben 86). Leipzig, 1931.

II. GENERAL WORKS

Strich, Fritz, Deutsche Klassik und Romantik oder Vollendung und Unendlichkeit: ein Versuch, 3. Auflage. München, 1928.

Korff, H. A., Geist der Goethezeit: Versuch einer ideellen Entwicklung der klassisch-romantischen Literaturgeschichte, I. Teil, "Sturm und Drang," II. Teil, "Klassik." Leipzig, 1923–30.

Kluckhohn, Paul, Persönlichkeit und Gemeinschaft: Studien zur Staatsauffassung der deutschen Romantik (Deutsche Vierteljahrsschrift für Literaturwissenschaft und Geistesgeschichte. Buchreihe, 5. Band). Halle, 1925. Reviewed by Kindermann, *Anzeiger*, XLVI, 58ff.; Rehm, *ZdPh*, LII, 491ff.

III. WORKS ON POLITICAL ROMANTICISM

Meinecke, Friedrich, Weltbürgertum und Nationalstaat: Studien zur Genesis des deutschen Nationalstaates, 3. Auflage. München, 1915.

Schmitt-Dorotic, Carl, Politische Romantik, München und Leipzig, 1919 (2. Auflage, 1925). Reviewed by Meinecke, *Hist. Zs.*, CXXI, 292ff.; Masur, *Hist. Zs.*, CXXXIV, 373ff.; Jordan, *Literaturblatt f. germ. u. roman. Phil.*, XLIII, 229ff.; Rothfels, *Deutsche Litztg.*, XLVII, 432ff.; Janentzky, *Logos*, XIV, 354ff.

Verschoor, A. D., Die ältere deutsche Romantik und die National-idee, Amsterdam, 1928 (Thesis, Groningen).

Schmitt-Dorotic, Carl, "Politische Theorie und Romantik," *Hist. Zs.*, CXXIII, 377ff.

Weinberger, Otto, "Romantik und Gesellschaftslehre," *Kölner Vjs. f. Soziol.*, V, 288ff.

Willoughby, L. A., "The Romantic Background of Hitlerism," *Contemporary Review*, CXLIV (1933), 682ff.

Novalis

Samuel, Richard, Die poetische Staats- und Geschichtsauffassung Fr. v. Hardenbergs (Deutsche Forschungen 12). Frankfurt a. M., 1925.

Adam Müller

Wolff, Karl, "Staat und Individuum bei Adam Müller: ein Beitrag zur Erforschung der romantischen Staatsphilosophie," *Hist. Vjs.*, XXX, 59ff.

Fichte

Engelbrecht, H. C., J. G. Fichte: a Study of His Political Writings. New York, 1933.

Heinsen, Marie, Individuum und Gemeinschaft bei Fichte. Dissertation, Erlangen, 1933.

Schenkel, E., Individualität und Gemeinschaft: der demokratische Gedanke bei Fichte. Zürich, 1933.

Hegel

Haering, Th. L., Gemeinschaft und Persönlichkeit in der Philosophie Hegels. Berlin, 1929.

Heller, H., Hegel und der nationale Machtstaatsgedanke in Deutschland. Berlin, 1921.

INDEX OF AUTHORS AND WORKS

N